The Production Assistant
in TV and Video

The Production Assistant in TV and Video

Avril Rowlands

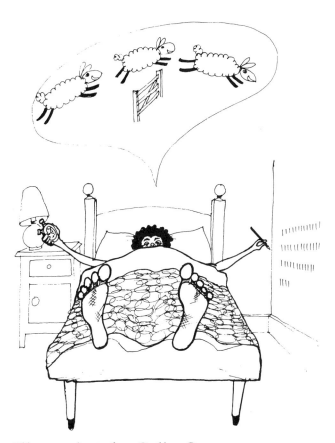

Illustrations by Colin Cant

ƒocal press

An imprint of Butterworth-Heinemann Ltd

2-92

Focal Press
An imprint of Butterworth-Heinemann Ltd
Linacre House, Jordan Hill, Oxford OX2 8DP

 PART OF REED INTERNATIONAL BOOKS

OXFORD LONDON BOSTON
MUNICH NEW DELHI SINGAPORE SYDNEY
TOKYO TORONTO WELLINGTON

First published, 1987
Reprinted 1991

British Library Cataloguing in Publication Data

Rowlands, Avril
    The production assistant in TV and Video
    I Television — Production and direction   II Video
    recordings — Production and direction
    I. Title
    791.45'0232   PN1992.75

ISBN 0 240 51255 3

Library of Congress Cataloguing in Publication Data

Rowlands, Avril
    The production assistant in tv and video
    1. Television — Production and direction. I. Title.
    II. Title: Production assistant in television and video
    PN1992.75.R6   1987   792'.0232'023   87-18328

ISBN 0 240 51255 3

Printed and Bound by Courier International Limited
East Kilbride

Contents

Acknowledgements   vii

A note to American readers   ix

1 Introduction   **1**
What is a production assistant?   3
A little bit of history   5

Part One   **Just keep counting: the 'live' PA**
The 'live' programme   10

2 News/topical current affairs   **12**
Components of programme   12
The organization of the newsroom   16
The running of the newsroom   19
Timing   26
The news script   32
The 'live' studio: just before transmission   40

3 Learn to love your stopwatch   **45**
Analogue and digital   45
Timing on air   48
Keep your head up! The importance of previewing   52
Rolling, cueing and counting   54
Studio discussions and interviews   58

4 Outside broadcasts   **61**
Involvement in programme content   61
Preparing for the OB   62
Living in the future   63
Importance to directors   63
Importance to camera operators   63
Importance to commentators   64
How to acquire that knowledge   64
Timing   65
Physical stamina   65
Communications   65
Leaving nothing to chance   66

5 Putting it all together   **68**
Dos and donts in the studio gallery   78
Hazards of the job   79

Part Two   **It'll be all right after it's edited: the flexible PA on recorded programmes**
Multi- and single camera shooting   86

6 In the beginning **89**
Initial paperwork 89
The production team 92
Wall charts, rehearsal scripts and schedules 95
The planning meeting and further programme requirements 102
Actors and rehearsals 105

7 The camera script **111**
Front pages 111
Studio recording order 113
The camera script: the body of the document 115
Camera script terms 123
Camera cards 126

8 The recording **128**
What to take 128
The studio floor 131
Gallery duties 133
Shot calling and timing 136
Time code logging 141
Light entertainment and music 145

9 Single camera shooting **152**
The schizophrenic PA 152
Preparing for location 154
Single camera shooting: continuity 157

10 Post-production and the PA **163**
Single camera shooting: information for the editor 163
Videotape editing 164
Sound 170
Clearing up 173

Part Three The wider world of television: the itinerant PA

11 The freelance PA **181**
Cable and satellite broadcasting 184
Pop promotions and commercials 187

Part Four Getting away from television: the non-broadcast PA

12 Non-broadcast use of videotape **193**
Industrial training 195
Education 199

Part Five All you ever wanted to know about videotape but were afraid to ask . . .

13 The PA's guide to videotape **205**
Sizes and formats of videotape 205
Television systems throughout the world 207

Index **209**

Acknowledgements

I am indebted to many individuals and companies for assistance with research into this book. Among them I would like to thank the Independent Television Companies Association for their generous support; also staff at BBC Pebble Mill, BBC Outside Broadcasts, Coventry Cable, Granada Television, ITN, Limelight Productions, Limehouse Studios, LWT, Shell Video Unit, Sky Channel, Sony Broadcast, Thames Television, TV-AM, TVS and the University of Birmingham Film Unit. I cannot list the many people from whom I received help, but I am most grateful to them all. Finally I must thank my husband, Christopher, who patiently reads everything I write and who has always been my best critic and adviser.

A note to American readers

Editor's note: The following information has been graciously provided by Judy Foy and her colleagues at WCVB-TV, Channel 5, Boston, Massachusetts.

Besides the differences in terminology (which will be covered in a glossary at the end of this section), there is one major difference between BBC-oriented British television and local commercial TV in the United States – at least, as far as the production assistant is concerned.

In the US, the role of the director seems to be more technical. The producer, along with his or her associates and assistants, deals more with the content of the programme.

In the UK, the production assistant takes on roles that would normally be performed by the director or the assistant director, for the most part, in the United States. Other tasks would usually be relegated solely to the producer or the associate producer of a show.

The widely varying influence of unionization in the US has led to many changes in the responsibilities of TV people. Also, the technological change associated with computerization has caused roles to alter rapidly. This has led to a certain fluidity in job content which seems to be at odds with the highly structured and detailed approach outlined in this book.

This is not to say that the book will not be useful to Americans. Indeed, it provides a body of knowledge that will more than prepare the reader for an entry-level job in broadcasting. However, a student or intern or beginning broadcasting professional will likely be frustrated and disappointed if he or she arrives at the station on the first day of work expecting to take on all the assignments described in this book. Rather, think of this as a 'thumbnail sketch' of what goes on administratively in the production of local programming.

Here, very roughly, is the administrative organizational chart for a local commercial American TV show:

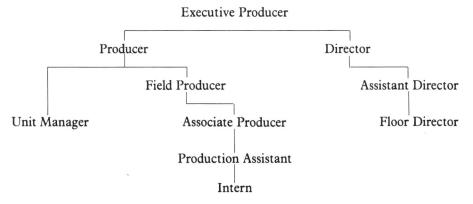

Glossary

British term	American equivalent
Big close up (BCU)	tight shot (TS)
Black edge generator (B/E)	drop shadow generator
Camera script	blocking script
Caption cards	art cards
Caption generator (capgen)	usually referred to as 'Kyron' or some other brand name of caption generator; sometimes loosely referred to as 'graphics'
Chat show	talk show
Closing title sequence	closing credits, credits
Crabbing	trucking
DFS	electronic still store (ESS)
DVE/Quantel	computer graphics, referred to by the brand name of the computer graphic generator
Floor manager	floor director
Gallery	control room
Gram	record
Ident	identification (ID)
'In' picture	first video
'In' word	incue
Inject	cut-in, remote
Insert	piece
Lace up	cue up
Lettering	superimposition, supers - e.g. Chyron
Link	copy leading up to a clip ('intro') or out to the next piece ('Outro', tag)
Location manager	field producer
Opting	feeding - i.e., 'we're waiting for a network feed . . .
Organizer	administrator, administrative assistant
Outside broadcast (OB)	remote
'Out' word	outcue, tag
Over-running	running long
Post Office line	telephone (land) line
Presentation	traffic department; master control; network
Presenter	newsreader, anchor
Production associate	associate producer
Production manager	unit manager
Production number	account number
Recce	reconnaissance
Rota	rotation
Run-up time	pre-roll time
Running order	format
Sequence	segment

SOT	sound on videotape
Source sheet	cut sheet
Standby	filler, filler piece
Straightforward	on-camera, O/C
Studio	studio session
Sub editor	copy editor
Sum	time
Superimposition	supers, lettering
Talkback	headset
Telecine	film
Teleprompt	prompter – both machine and operator
Tracking	dollying
Transmission monitor	air monitor
Under-running	running short
Venue	place, location
Vet	edit
Vision mixer	switcher – both machine and operator
VTR	videotape

1

Introduction

There you sit, in a darkened control gallery of the studio, a pencil grasped tightly in your slightly damp and decidedly nervous hand, your eyes fixed on the running order as you try to make sense of the row of figures down the page.

On one side of you sits the producer who leans across - wafting unmistakeable signs of stress - and monopolizes your space, your nose and your telephone.

On your other side, the director twitches uncontrollably and picks up one of your four stopwatches (one master watch, one insert watch and two 'just in case'), thus displacing the neatly regimented row which you had just laid out. You feel a moment's irrational anger, elbow the producer out of the way and offer the director a mint humbug which he accepts with all the desperation of a man who has just run out of cigarettes.

You return to your figures, but your concentration is gone and you replace your stopwatch - having wrested it from the director - into its former position and re-align it together with your running order, your script, blank sheets of paper, ruler, eraser, coloured pens, pencils and the three other watches, into the rigidly precise pattern which is your attempt to impose security upon an insecure environment.

You raise your eyes and are confronted by a battery of television monitors. The sight is both alarming and confusing so you return to your figures.

'How much?' hisses the producer, leaning over your shoulder. You edge away, but that brings you into too close a proximity with the director so you move back.

'Er . . . two minutes over . . .' you say, hoping that the producer will not want you to be too precise.

The producer studies your running order and decides to cut down on the time allotted to the first interview. You depress the key on the desk in order to pass this information directly to the presenter in the studio and incur thereby the wrath of the director who is giving instructions to the camera operators and dislikes others talking at the same time. You return to checking your timings then glance up at the studio clock.

'Five minutes to transmission, five minutes,' you say.

The floor manager informs the director that the Important Person who is to be interviewed as the first item in the programme has not yet arrived. The floor assistant is sent hot-foot to find out what has happened while the director relieves his feelings by swearing at you, at interviewees who are late and at the world in general.

The vision mixer, who has been placidly knitting throughout, pushes a packet of cigarettes towards the director which acts as a temporary palliative but infuriates the studio supervisor who, having recently given up smoking has, with all the zeal of the convert, banished the ashtrays from the gallery.

The director flicks ash into your polystyrene cup of coffee while you, reflecting fleetingly upon the Jekyll and Hyde character of directors for whom you have worked, fail to notice the flashing white light.

'Telephone,' says the studio supervisor sourly, his nostrils twitching at the aroma of cigarette smoke.

You answer the telephone and are informed that the Important Person has just arrived at reception in an advanced state of intoxication. You pass on the message and are rewarded by more invective from the director and a homily from the studio supervisor on the evils of drink – he is a confirmed tee-totaller as well. The vision mixer shakes her head comfortably and continues to knit.

'Are we going to rehearse the opening?' asks an anxious voice, which is disregarded by the director as he is trying out some complicated electronic effects for possible use later on in the programme.

You, meanwhile, are fully engrossed with marking up fresh pages of script which have just arrived, altering your timings and taking a message from an over-anxious telecine operator who is worried that the film needed for Sequence 10 has not arrived. As the film is not needed until the second half of the programme, you provide the necessary reassurance. Then you hear from presentation that your programme is to go on the air earlier than planned. Your heart begins to pound and your mouth goes dry as you glance at the studio clock.

'Two minutes to transmission, two minutes.'

'Have to speak up love,' says a disembodied voice.

You apologize as the director abandons the electronic effects in favour of the more pressing need to rehearse the opening titles. The floor manager reports that the Important Person is being sick in the dressing room and the director abandons the opening titles in order to confer with the producer in view of the interviewee's state of health.

The director suggests starting with Sequence 6. That is vetoed by the producer who suggests Sequence 10. You – sandwiched uncomfortably in the middle – point out that the film required for Sequence 10 is not yet ready. The director asks why not and you avoid answering by suggesting that you start with Sequence 3. The suggestion is ignored. The director jabs his finger down your running order, the producer digs you in the ribs and, feeling rather like the Dormouse at the Mad Hatter's tea-party, you glance at the studio clock.

'One minute to transmission, one minute.'

The director decides to start with Sequence 3 and is just informing the studio when the wan figure of the Important Person is to be seen in the monitor. A joyful floor manager guides him to his seat, gently sits him down and tenderly clips a microphone to his tie.

'Forty-five seconds to transmission, forty-five seconds.'

Butterflies are doing a war dance in your stomach and you fight down an urgent desire to go to the lavatory.

'Stand by VTR with opening titles.'

You pick up two of your stopwatches. They feel cold in your clammy hands.

'What are we starting with?' wails the teleprompt operator.

'Thirty seconds to transmission, thirty seconds.'

The vision mixer calmly puts aside her knitting, puts on her spectacles and looks up attentively while the director runs through the opening sequences.

Your eyes are fixed on the studio clock and the transmission monitor which is showing the closing credits of the preceding programme.

'Fifteen seconds.'

There must be an easier way of earning a living, you think, as the adrenalin pumps through your body and your heart beats in slow, heavy thumps.

'10 . . . 9 . . . 8 . . . 7 . . . 6 . . . ROLL VTR! . . . 4 . . . 3 . . . 2 . . . 1 . .'

You start both stopwatches.

'On air . . .'

The butterflies have ceased, your hands are steady as you place your master stopwatch on the desk and pick up a red pen. Your voice is calm and clear.

There you sit, cool, competent, in control. A complete Production Assistant.

'There you sit, cool, competent, in control. A complete Production Assistant.'

What is a production assistant?

A production assistant is someone who works in television or the communications industry as an essential part of the production team. The PA is, in essence, the director's personal assistant and is usually involved at every stage of production from start to finish. It is a demanding, challenging and immensely satisfying job as it lies at the organizational heart of any production.

The job can comprise some or all of a number of different elements which can roughly be divided into three separate strands:

Organizational

'The organizing skills of a General – and a good one at that – together with the patience of a Saint' is how I have heard this facet of the PA's job described. The organizational role of the PA means acting as the administrative core of the production – the spider at the centre of the web.

Now this might not be true of all productions. The larger the production the more personnel there will be performing functions which, on smaller shows would fall under the sole jurisdiction of the PA. But there is a greater or lesser amount of administration and organization required in all PA's work, hand in hand with good secretarial skills, a methodical approach and an ability to liaise and communicate with people at all levels. The organizational side of a PA's job will overlap with the other strands of the work and require no specialized training other than that for any good secretary.

Location work on film or video

The second strand to a PA's job is that of continuity when involved in out-of-sequence, single camera shooting, most usually on film but also increasingly now on videotape.

The job of continuity is a highly specialized one and is fully covered in my book, *Script Continuity and the Production Secretary.*

Studio work

This book is essentially about the no less specialized 'electronic' side of the PA's job – the vital role she plays in the control room or gallery of a studio when working on live and recorded programmes.

This is the third strand of the PA's work and involves a certain technical knowledge and expertise, fast and accurate time-keeping and the ability to work under intense pressure. The specific tasks of timing, shot calling, rolling in pre-recorded items, time-code logging and general communications are skills that are specifically related to this branch of the PA's work and as such have to be learnt before the PA can cope with a studio gallery unaided. There is also the organizational side of studio work, the camera scripts, running orders, camera cards, etc. which need to be understood.

All things . . .

Some people would answer the question 'What is a Production Assistant?' by saying that a PA is all things to all men – or, presumably 'women' in these liberated days! Yet others would say that PAs are nothing but glorified secretaries.

The aim of this book is neither to glorify nor to denigrate the job of the Production Assistant. What it will attempt to do is to work through the 'electronic' side, the studio side of the PA's job not just in television but also in the vastly expanding areas that are beginning to realize and make use of the scope and potential of videotape: in industrial training, in education, in production companies other than mainstream television.

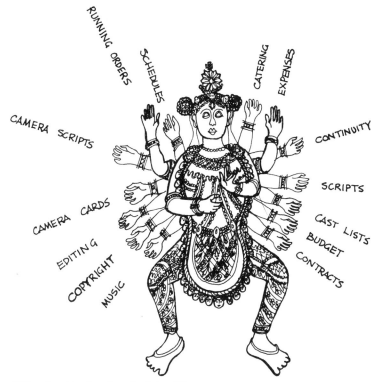

Around the figure, clockwise from top: RUNNING ORDERS, SCHEDULES, CATERING, EXPENSES, CONTINUITY, SCRIPTS, CAST LISTS, BUDGET, CONTRACTS, MUSIC, COPYRIGHT, EDITING, CAMERA CARDS, CAMERA SCRIPTS

'What is a Production Assistant?'

But this is not a book about television or video *per se*. It is about that complex creature working in a complex medium who needs a galaxy of skills as well as a cast iron constitution in order to cope with the requirements of the job – the requirements of being a PA.

Note

Throughout the book I have referred to the production assistant as *she*. This is not for any sexist reason but because in the UK the job is more commonly done by a woman. As there is not a suitable pronoun referring equally to *he* and *she*, I hope I will be forgiven for that and for any other apparent stereotypes. They are not intended.

A little bit of history

The early days

In these days, when many people have video recorders in their own homes, it is important to remember that for many years after the British Broadcasting Corporation started the first public television service in the world in 1936, all programmes were either live or on film and were, of course, in black and white as were most cinema feature films except for the most lavish.

Live television

Nowadays we tend to take television for granted. The fact that we can see, from the comfort of our armchair, a football match that is being played at that moment on the other side of the world and conveyed to us by satellite is something we all accept. But in the early days it was thought of as something totally magical and its popularity spread rapidly.

To begin with almost everything was transmitted live, not just the news, sport, current affairs and magazine-type programmes that we are accustomed to. A studio drama, for example, would be rehearsed and then transmitted – beginning at the beginning and going on to the end. If it was to be repeated then the whole production would be remounted in the studio at some later date. Any mistakes would be seen by the entire viewing audience. If something went drastically wrong, the only outlet was for the caption *NORMAL SERVICE WILL BE RESUMED AS SOON AS POSSIBLE* to be shown.

People still sigh for the 'golden' days of television. They say it lent an element of excitement and adventure which is altogether lacking from pre-recorded programmes and many actors feel that their performances were given a definite edge in the knowledge that they were being seen, live, by audiences of thousands – soon increasing to millions. There have been attempts to recreate live drama with mixed success. Television has moved on and both audiences and programmes have grown so sophisticated that attempts to turn back the clock are not really viable.

Film recording

In the early 1950s it was obvious that there was a great need for recording television programmes, and a system of film recording was devised. A specially designed film camera with a magazine holding up to one hour of film was set up in front of a high quality TV monitor and the pictures literally filmed off the screen.

Its advantage was that it could go through the same post production in terms of editing and dubbing as a film and it was also valuable as a means of retaining live programmes which would otherwise have been lost.

Its disadvantages were that:

(a) it was expensive;
(b) the film recording (sometimes known as a *kinescope*) had to go through the processing stage in the laboratories which was time consuming; and
(c) on transmission through a telecine channel there was a marked loss of picture quality.

The advent of videotape

It was not until the late 1950s/early 1960s that the use of videotape began to revolutionize television although experiments in magnetic recording had been going on for years before that.

For the first time programmes could be stored on tape and, unlike film recording, could be transmitted and repeated at any time without loss of picture quality. A library could be organized and programmes kept – if not for posterity for the optimum life of videotape is still unknown – at least for a considerable number of years.

But perhaps the greatest advantage of videotape lay in the speed with which one could put together a programme comprising many different source elements and get it on the air. This opened up far greater possibilities for programme making especially as the initially primitive editing facilities improved.

During the past few years the technological revolution in all areas of video with the lighter, more versatile cameras and the advances in complex computerized editing has provided fresh scope in programme making.

Television today

Television today can be immensely complex. The ingredients in any one programme can be obtained from a number of different sources and the PA needs an overall understanding of the processes involved and her own specific job in helping to weld the many components into a single production.

This book

In this book I have divided television in a fairly arbitrary way into two main elements: live and pre-recorded. These two elements will then be subdivided as necessary. I have settled on these two main elements mainly because the work of the PA,

'To begin with, almost everything was transmitted live.'

although freely spilling over into each area, does contain certain different priorities whether one is working on live or pre-recorded programmes.

So as television itself started as a live medium, we shall also, and examine the vital role of the 'live' PA.

Part One
Just keep counting: the 'live' PA

The 'live' programme

The demands of the job

The role of the Production Assistant in the gallery of a programme that is being transmitted live is one that is often technically very demanding. It carries with it a weight of responsibility and requires coolness, concentration and the ability to work under extremes of pressure. An aptitude for fast, accurate mental arithmetic is a definite advantage.

Responsibilities of the job

The job can be summed up in general terms by stating that a PA's function on a live show is to get the programme off the air cleanly and on time, but to say that is an over-simplification, for the PA is responsible for a good deal more besides, namely:

- [ ] taking overall and insert timings in order that the producer may be able to allocate the requisite time for each individual item within the total duration of the programme;
- [ ] being the central point of communication both for receiving and disseminating information;
- [ ] liaising with network control to get on and off the air smoothly;
- [ ] taking in changes while on the air and adjusting timings accordingly;
- [ ] keeping everyone connected with the programme informed as to the point reached on the running order or script by means of verbal idents and shot calling;
- [ ] giving warning standbys to those who require it, e.g. presenters, grams, VTR and telecine channel operators and so on;
- [ ] providing a smooth transition from live to pre-recorded material and back by means of accurate time counts;
- [ ] acting as a verbal clock, giving countdowns to presenters and timings to the end of each individual item and to the end of the programme;
- [ ] bar counting where musical items are involved.

The Production Assistant may be required to do all or only some of these things and possibly has other responsibilities during the gallery which I have not listed, depending on the nature and content of the programme. Many of the same jobs are also required of the PA on pre-recorded programmes, but if the show is live, there is the heightened tension, the knowledge that mistakes cannot afterwards be edited out but will be seen by the entire viewing public. This thought makes many experienced PAs shy away from the thought of doing a live show, but it also gives the extra edge, the added excitement and the attraction for other PAs which they find lacking in pre-recorded programmes. The fact that once the programme is over it is totally finished with is another bonus. Mistakes are soon forgotten and there is little clearing up and the minimum of paperwork.

Types of programme

The kinds of programmes that are likely to be transmitted live can be roughly grouped as follows:

1. News.
2. Current Affairs – topical programmes, perhaps examining items of news or a controversial issue in depth with presenters and studio discussions with experts and/or audience participation. In addition, there might be pre-recorded inserts.
3. Magazine-type programmes which could contain all sorts of ingredients: music, dancing, cookery, fashion, sport, interviews with personalities, possibly updates on news, often with fairly long pre-recorded items linked by a presenter live in the studio.
4. Sport – generally an outside broadcast.
5. Large single event – usually an outside broadcast. This could range from large State occasion to a variety show or a charity event.

These programmes all vary in content and in complexity, but they do all have one thing in common. When the PA is sitting next to the director in the studio gallery or outside broadcast control room, counting down to transmission, outwardly calm and in control, her heart will nonetheless be pounding away, her mouth dry, the palms of her hands will be damp and adrenalin will be pumping round her system at overtime rate.

What is also certain is that once on air these symptoms will cease. And it has been truly said that if a PA stops having these symptoms, it is time she gave up working on live shows. Live programmes are hard, exacting and demanding, but they do have their own excitement and for those PAs and would be PAs who wish for that kind of stimulation, or who have to work 'live' whether or not they enjoy it, we will examine the work involved.

'Outwardly calm and in control . . .'

2

News/topical current affairs

Components of programme

Before we examine the PAs work in the live news-type programme, we ought perhaps to look at the different elements that go to make up that programme. These can be roughly itemized as follows:

1. Presenter(s)/Newsreader(s)

No news, current affairs or magazine-type programme would be complete without the presenter (or newsreader, linkman or anchorman or whatever he/she is called). There may be one, two or even more on a programme and their role is crucial in introducing the different items, providing smooth links from one story to another, conducting interviews or giving live voice-over commentaries to pre-recorded inserts. In other words, they hold the programme together.

They are highly professional people and as time-conscious as the PA. The consistency of their speed of delivery is vital as inserts are cued in according to the duration of their links and, providing the PA in the gallery has done her work correctly, the presenter bears a great responsibility for the smooth transition between items. They may, and frequently are, called upon while on air, to ad lib for a length of time in order to pad an under-running programme or, conversely, to cut down on prepared links to save time if over-running. A good presenter is invaluable to a PA and a good PA is a life-line to a presenter.

So, if the presenter is the first component in this type of programme, the next must be

2. Pre-recorded inserts

News stories are gathered in various ways, by agencies, by 'our man on the spot', by events that have been ear-marked long before by the producer, by a number of other means. Most of them end up injected into the live programme as pre-recorded, edited inserts and originate from different sources:

12

(a) Film (telecine)

Usually shot on 16mm film. The film would then be played into the programme through a telecine channel or might be transferred to videotape for transmission.

(b) Videotape (ENG)

The material recorded on a professional video cassette machine either on three quarter or half inch videotape cassettes. If this material is edited on to a similar format cassette as opposed to being transferred to full size videotape, it is played directly into the programme from a video cassette recorder. For the purposes of this section of the book I will refer to it as ENG although some companies use different names, e.g. PSC. For a more detailed explanation of different formats of videotape see Chapter 13.

(c) Videotape (VTR)

The material might have been recorded or compiled on a video recorder using one or two inch tape. For the purposes of this book I will call this VTR.

3. Live

There might be live injects coming from other studio centres or OB units. These live injections are very difficult to schedule accurately in the overall running order of a programme, very often because a news story is just about to break or has just broken.

A classic example of this is of a news bulletin extended to give live coverage of the arrival of a plane containing some important person. A cold reporter, shivering on the tarmac of the airfield ad libs his way through ten minutes of agonized waiting because the plane has been delayed. The cameraman shows us shots of everything he can find in his viewfinder, whether or not it bears any relationship to the subject. The wait continues. At last the director cuts back to the studio and at that precise moment the plane lands. Live programmes are unpredictable if nothing else!

4. Graphics

A fourth and most important element of any news/topical current affairs type programme is that of graphic design.

The increasing use of computers and new technology with specialized electronic effects has over the last few years made a tremendous impact in the field of graphic design.

The range and scope of advanced computerized effects are staggering and it is easy to become confused and uncertain of what and how different effects can be achieved.

Because this book is primarily for PAs and because it is the PA who will most probably have to book facilities and liaise with the graphic design department, I will briefly work through the graphic design element in any programme, whether live or recorded.

(a) Lettering (end credits and name superimpositions)

Every single production will need lettering of some sort, even if it is only the end credits. Lettering is the basic bread and butter of graphic design.

Lettering can be achieved in the following ways:

  (i)   By means of dry transfer lettering, e.g. Letraset, which is stuck on to caption cards and then recorded or transmitted straight from the studio. The obvious difficulty with this system is that a number of studio cameras will inevitably be tied up in the process.

  (ii) Captions with lettering can be photographed and made into 35mm transparencies. These slides are placed in the correct order in a slide projector and cued into the studio at the appropriate moments. The vision mixer changes the transparencies from the control desk.

  (iii) End credits can be in the form of a paper roller made up of Letraset names. This might then be recorded in the studio.

  (iv) Lettering can be achieved by means of computers known as character generators. These machines provide a comprehensive video lettering service capable of producing lettering in a variety of typeface, size, shape and colouring.

The lettering can either be assembled and edited in advance of the studio and stored on disc, or an operator can type up the letters in the gallery of the studio for recording or transmission if live.

In addition to lettering, many computers will produce logos and symbols. A 'house' style can be worked out for each programme with an overall design of logos, symbols and type face. The design for each programme can be stored on floppy disc.

Most television companies refer to captions created from character generators by the trade name of the system chosen by each company, e.g. Aston, Capgen etc. For the purpose of this book I shall call them 'capgens'.

(b) Captions (maps, diagrams, photographs recorded in the studio)

Many productions require maps, diagrams or still photographs. At their simplest, these would be mounted on to caption cards and recorded or transmitted from the studio. A less wasteful process would be to photograph the mounted captions and make 35mm transparencies. Alternatively, the captions could be recorded using a rostrum mounted video camera.

Specialized computers can now store, re-touch, re-size and re-position captions as well as present them in the required order. As the scope of these computers embrace more than just maps, diagrams and still photographs, we will look at them in conjunction with the next element in graphic design.

(c) Creative sequences (titles, animations, inserts, promotional trailers)

This is the main-stream work of the design department and each job usually demands innovation and originality. Each job is therefore by definition different. There are various computers now on the market which help both in the creation and the storage of the work and which can make hitherto impossible effects both simply and easily achieved.

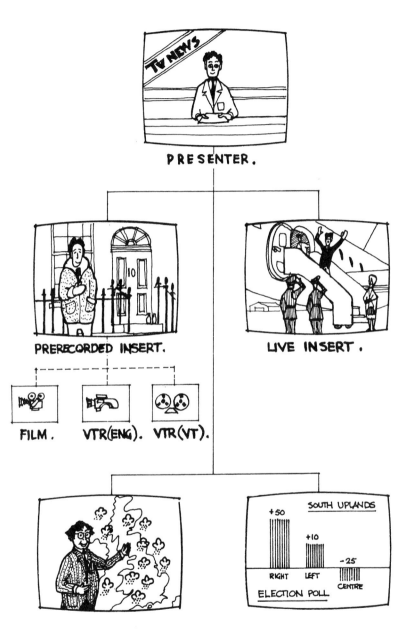

PRESENTER.

PRERECORDED INSERT.   LIVE INSERT.

FILM.   VTR(ENG).   VTR(VT).

GRAPHICS.

Components of the news/topical/current affairs programme.

There are computers designed for creating fine art and graphics, rather like an electronic version of paint, paper, paste, scissors, card and stencil to the graphic artist. There are electronic systems providing some or all of the following: multiple pictures; borders and matte effects; images at any size from normal to virtually zero; wipes; split screens; flips; cubes; re-sizing and re-positioning of still pictures. All these effects can be recorded and stored. Then there are frame stores which electronically store any picture in whatever order is selected by the operator.

But it must be remembered however that all these computers are specialist machines with fixed software programmes. They are ultimately as good or as bad as the graphic artist who operates them. In order to make the fullest and most creative use of these computers it is essential that the graphic designers be involved at an early stage in the programme.

Film programmes

Traditionally graphics on an all-film programme were created by filming the art work and then arranging for the film laboratory to optically superimpose this on the background pictures. There is, however, an increasing tendency to complete the programme on film as far as a fully graded transmission print and then run it through a telecine channel with electronic art work superimposed at the relevant points and recorded on videotape. Thus a programme entirely originated on film is eventually transmitted from a VTR channel.

The organization of the newsroom

If one wanders into a television newsroom it looks, in layout, very like the busy newsroom of any newspaper with its telex and printout machines from news agencies, its banks of telephones, typewriters, newspapers, photographs, and the constant chatter and bustle of a room full of busy people. The main difference being that in a television newsroom there is at least one, if not more, television set mounted in a prominent place, permanently switched on even if the sound is turned down.

It can appear chaotic and disorganized – the kind of place where typewriters have to be chained to their desks lest they mysteriously 'walk' overnight, where 'I need it *now*' means that it is an hour overdue, and where everyone looks as if they are living on their nerves, their gastric ulcers and their stale, two-week old sandwiches, the smell of which permeates the room. It can, conversely, appear organized and ordered, but appearances are, in any event, deceptive.

Leaving aside the environment therefore, let us look at the people:

Producer of the day

Under the overall control of the head of the department or the series editor comes the producer of the day (who might also be called programme editor). He or she is basically responsible for the programme content, for the placing of each item in the running order and for the length of time allotted to it. The producer, under the overall department head, has the final say on editorial content.

There might, in addition, be a chief sub editor, whose basic job is to vet the journalists' reports.

Reporters/journalists

There will be a number of reporters/journalists and researchers. Their brief is to cover whatever is newsworthy, research into it, report on it and present their item in packaged form for the programme. Their sphere of operations covers a wide range.

Programme director

His or her job is to wield together the many components of the programme into a whole during transmission. There will probably be a number of directors who will work on a rota basis.

Organizers/clerks

The terms 'organizer' or 'clerk' is only used in some companies. In others this function is covered by people as diverse as secretaries and station assistants and their duties may range from booking any kind of facility that is required – studios, video and telecine channels, graphics, post office lines – to arranging the travel details of reporters and crews, or obtaining, sorting and mounting stills and so on.

It is difficult in this book to delineate precisely the exact responsibilities of different people working on productions as each television company and each programme has a different way of delegating the work. But it is true to say that many of the jobs that would be the responsibility of the PA in other areas of television production are, in the live news-type programme, given to others. This is because of the special demands the live gallery makes upon the PA. The heavier the demands in terms of the amount and accuracy of the timing, the less involvement the PA has with any aspect of the programme content.

Teleprompt operator

The teleprompt operator is the person who types the scripts for whatever teleprompt system is used in the studio. In some companies where computers are used in the newsroom, the job is occasionally done by a PA. Autocue, Portaprompt, Digiprompt, are all trade names for the device which is mounted on to a studio camera enabling the presenter to read an enlarged image of the script while apparently looking directly at the viewer. The term 'teleprompt' will be used throughout this book.

Production assistant

The number of production assistants working on any particular programme of this type can vary from one to six or more, with a possible back-up team of typists and secretaries. The rota of work likewise varies. If the programme goes out nightly, there might be a total of three PAs alternating the work on a rota basis. One would do the gallery, one would act as co-ordinator and runner for the gallery PA and the third would clear up last night's work, sort out costings, music details, contracts, invoices and so on.

DEPARTMENT HEAD.

PRODUCER.

CHIEF SUB EDITOR.

REPORTERS/JOURNALISTS.

PROGRAMME DIRECTOR.

ORGANISERS/CLERKS.

TELEPROMPT OPERATOR.

PRODUCTION ASSISTANTS.

TYPISTS/SECRETARIES.

The organization of the newsroom.

A fourth PA might help type scripts if this job is not undertaken by typists or done by computer. The PAs tend to work as a team, assisting one another at times of intense pressure.

Typists/secretaries

These might be employed to type the script if this is not the responsibility of the PA. They do any other typing, they might book facilities and anything else needful. Their work frequently overlaps that of the PA and the organizers/clerks in the field of pure administration.

The running of the newsroom

During the morning

If we follow through a day in the life of a PA on a fairly typical news-type programme, we might envisage the following schedule:

Early morning conference
Early in the day there will be a meeting between the producer of the day, the director of that evening's programme and the journalists. This meeting would be to throw ideas around, to check work in progress and to list who does what. If pre-recordings are to be made, possibly an interview or the putting together of some composite package, this would be noted by the director. The PA might or might not attend this meeting.

Throughout the day news items will come in from various sources. Those items are edited, links written, photographs and name superimpositions acquired. The PA might be involved in the administration of some or all of this but more likely it will be delegated to others. That does not mean that the PA has an easy time of it however, for the gallery PA's work really begins with the next meeting, which for our fictitious programme will be at 2.00 pm.

Planning meeting
At this meeting the draft running order is given out by the producer. He or she will list the items, state, as far as is known at this stage, the technical requirements needed, the source from which the items will be generated, the placing of the item in the programme – although this, as everything, may well change – and the length of time the producer has, provisionally, allotted to that item. Any information the producer has will be fed into the meeting and the journalists will report on the stages their items have reached. From this information the PA will add up a rough overall timing and type out a draft running order, to be printed on coloured paper and circulated.

Computer
Some newsrooms are now computerized, which has done away with much of the typing of scripts and running orders. Using a centrally linked computer, reporters write their stories directly on the computer keyboard. These stories are read by the producer and the presenter from the VDU and any changes made before it is printed out in script form. The running order is also compiled on the computer by the PA. It can be updated and changed throughout the day before being printed out just before the programme. Some computers time the links and print the figure on the running order, but these should be re-checked by the PA as they can be inaccurate.

'Some newsrooms are now computerized.'

The running order

Each programme has its own format for setting out a running order, one which is easily understood and acceptable to everyone working on the programme. Some programmes like as much information as possible put down on the running order, others like the barest minimum. The example given on page 22 shows the following:

General details

The programme title, the date and programme number have been shown. The running time (R/T) together with the 'on air' and 'off air' times have also been typed in although these might be approximations at this stage.

The names of the key personnel have been shown, implying that these might vary from day to day.

Sequences

Every programme, whether live or pre-recorded is, at some stage or other, broken down into small, manageable segments. Because live programmes contain elements from many different sources it breaks down neatly into different sections that are placed in an order pre-determined by the producer of the day and linked by the presenter.

Each numbered sequence shown on the running order therefore consists of a separate story together with its link into or out of it. In the example on page 22, the only exception is Sequence 5, where three short news items have been placed together under the overall title 'Shorts'.

The final order may well change and some PAs leave gaps to allow for the addition of possible late items, thus spreading the thirteen items listed over numbers ranging from 1 to 20.

Source

The next column relates to the source from which the item originates.

Sequence 1 is a pre-recorded opening title sequence on videotape before coming to the studio to see the two presenters on cameras 1 and 2. The sources therefore for Sequence 1 would be VTR and studio.

Sequence 2 shows a studio link into the item 'Lost Children'. The cameras involved will be 1 and 3, camera 3 showing a photograph which will be overlaid on camera 1's shot of the presenter. 'Lost Children' comes from an ENG source and name superimpositions (CAPS) will be timed in by the PA.

Sequence 3 sees another studio link into the item on 'New Technology'. Camera will be giving us a shot of the presenter while camera 4 will overlay the relevant still photograph. 'New Technology' comes from a VTR source and is now a composite package from an original film together with a pre-recorded studio interview. Name superimpositions are to be added.

Sequence 4 is a straightforward link into an ENG item.

Sequence 5, 'Shorts', consists of brief news items on film, tape and film respectively. The film items are mute and will require voice-over commentary by the studio presenters on cues given by the PA or floor manager.

Sequence 6 is a short 'Tease', a preview of the item on 'Hidden Treasure' which comes later in the programme. The sequence is to be pre-recorded in the studio during the afternoon.

Sequences 7, 8, 9 and 10 are straightforward.

Sequence 11 is also to be pre-recorded during the afternoon.

The closing headlines, Sequence 12, shows us the two presenters in the studio with insets on cameras 3 and 4.

The closing sequence, 13, has a last comment and goodnights from the presenters on cameras 1 and 2 before going into the closing title sequence recorded on VTR.

Title/presenter/reporter

The next column gives the name of the story, the initials of the reporter responsible and the presenter who is to give the link for the item.

Durations

If no durations are known at this stage, this column could be left out. If there are only one or two known durations these could be typed in and other figures added as they are made available to the PA. Alternatively, this column could be used for the producer's estimated times. In the following example, the producer's estimated times are shown in brackets and the known times without brackets.

The durations for each sequence are, of course, made up of two, if not three, separate timings:

(a) the duration of the link into the item;
(b) the duration of the pre-recorded insert;
(c) a possible back-up link out of the item.

```
DRAFT RUNNING ORDER      :       WEEKDAY NEWS    :    WEDNESDAY 1 MAY 1985

In:   18.00.00                    Programme Number: XYZ/1234/A
R/T:    20.25
Out:  18.20.25


Producer  :  Mary Jones               Presenters:   Cherry Stone
Director  :  Dougal McLean                           Andrew Plum
P.A       :  Josie Blane
F.M       :  Fred Smith
```

SEQ.	SOURCE	TITLE/PRES/REP	EST. DURATION
1	VTR STUDIO (1&2)	TITLES Cherry & Andrew	0.23 (0.30)
2	STUDIO (1/3)+CAP ENG + CAPS	Cherry links to LOST CHILDREN (TW)	(2.35)
3	STUDIO (2/4)+CAP VTR + CAPS	Andrew links to NEW TECHNOLOGY (PT)	(2.20)
4	STUDIO (1) ENG + CAPS	Cherry links to SOCCER VIOLENCE (LW)	(1.15)
5	STUDIO (1/2) TELECINE (Mute) VTR + CAPS TELECINE (Mute)	Andrew & Cherry /SHORTS/ HOUSING PROJECT LOIS GREY BARN MURDER	 (2.45)
6	VTR	TEASE : HIDDEN TREASURE	(0.15)
7	STUDIO (2/3)+CAP ENG + CAPS	Andrew links to WAR CRIMES (CP)	(2.10)
8	STUDIO (1/4)+CAP VTR + CAPS	Cherry links to STATE VISIT (LE)	(1.25)
9	STUDIO (2) TELECINE + CAPS	Andrew links to HIDDEN TREASURE (AB)	1.55
10	STUDIO (2/3)+CAP ENG + CAPS	Andrew links to SPORT	(2.35)
11	STUDIO (1) VTR	Cherry links to WEATHER	(1.15)
12	STUDIO (1/2) (3/4) + CAPS	CLOSING HEADLINES Cherry and Andrew	(0.35)
13	STUDIO (1&2) VTR	AND FINALLY..Cherry GOODNIGHT (C & A) PROG. CLOSE	 (0.35) 0.15

```
STANDBYS:   RAIN FORESTS (TP)      2'10"
            INDUSTRIAL REVIVAL (CP) 1'10"
```

Example of a draft running order.

These can be shown separately and only added together in the later columns which the PA fills in.

Space could be left on the righthand side of the running order for the PA to work out the cumulative times, or this might be done on a separate sheet, a time chart, according to preference.

Standbys

The standbys are completed items which might need to be slotted in at the last minute if the programme is under-running or if another item is not ready in time.

Estimates

Having just completed and distributed the draft running order, it becomes clear that, at this stage of the proceedings, all the timings other than the opening and closing titles and Sequence 9 in our programme are *estimates* only, given by the producer, who arrived at them in the following way:

(a) Firstly, on the basis of the information given at the 2.00 pm meeting, but it must be remembered that at this stage the stories had not been edited.
(b) Secondly, by the producer's own feelings about the worth, in terms of screen time, of each item.

It cannot be said too often that any item might be changed, dropped, shortened or lengthened at any time until the programme is off the air. In the event of a major news item breaking, the entire proposed running order might be scrapped.

During the afternoon

The following things happen at no specified times during the afternoon:

1. Pre-recordings

The director makes any necessary pre-recordings in the studio. This may involve the services of the gallery PA or some other PA, who will then pass on the following information to the gallery PA:

(a) duration of pre-recorded item, and
(b) the 'in' and 'out' words and picture.

2. Completion of items

Journalists will be busy editing and dubbing their own individual stories. Once completed it is, in theory, either their responsibility or the responsibility of the film or VTR editor to give the PA the following information for that item:

(a) duration of item;
(b) the 'in' and 'out' words and picture;
(c) details of name superimpositions and the timing at which they should occur;
(d) if known, which channel is to play the item into the programme;
(e) any music or other copyright details.

But frequently journalists and film and VTR editors are hard enough pressed to make the deadline of transmission without worrying about information for the PA. It then falls on the PA to chase up these details.

3. Graphics

During the afternoon, captions will be mounted, stills and photographs acquired, maps and charts sorted and all these will be compiled in the correct order for the programme.

4. Capgens

A list of capgens will be made and given to the operator, again in the correct order.

5. Links

As items are edited, the presenter's links will be written and passed to the PAs or secretaries for typing, unless a computer is used. These links, once they have been passed by the producer and the presenter, form the basis of the script.

6. Teleprompt

As the script is duplicated, a copy must be passed to the teleprompt operator.

7. Floor plan

The director will work out his camera and boom positions within the studio set and plot them on a floor plan. (See Chapter 6 for illustration of a floor plan.)

The pace hots up

From mid-afternoon onwards in the newsroom the pace increases as the transmission time draws near. As the afternoon progresses the gallery PA will, hopefully, be able to add to her running order or time chart the *real*, as opposed to the *estimated* timings, and keep an eye on the real running time as opposed to the estimated one.

At 5.00 pm the final running order is typed, duplicated – usually on different coloured paper from the draft – and distributed.

The PA's job

The gallery PA is very much at the centre of all this activity. She is the one who, in many ways, holds the various threads together. She is the central point of contact, constantly being given information, assimilating it, passing it on to those who need it and, above all, keeping a keen eye on the overall timing of the programme as the timings of the individual items become finalized.

It is useful, but not standard practice, for the gallery PA to sit with the producer and director during the afternoon as the accent is on fast, accurate communication between these three people.

Liaison

The key to the gallery PA's job during the run-up to the programme is liaison. Liaison with the producer and director throughout the afternoon is essential both to keep them aware of changes as they are brought to her attention and to keep up to date with the fluctuations of the overall duration.

That is not to say that the PA will run to the producer every time her sums make the programme five seconds or so light or heavy, but in a programme of, say,

'From mid-afternoon onwards in the newsroom the pace increases as the transmission time draws near.'

twenty minutes length, the producer will want to know if it is running around two minutes over or under. Exactly when to bother the producer is very much a matter of experience and of having an understanding of the content of the items.

Communication is a two-way process, however, and it is right for the PA to expect to be kept informed of any changes planned by the producer or director during the run-up to the programme.

Timing

But above all, the PA working on live, fast, news-type programmes must be able to add up and subtract time quickly and accurately, especially when it is only one minute to transmission and a flood of completed items with their durations is handed in – and some PAs would say that if the information comes in one minute before transmission it is going to be a relaxed show!

Timing

Whether you do your sums on your running order or make a separate time chart, what you, the PA, are essentially doing is keeping a check on the real timings as they are given to you, comparing them with the producer's estimated ones, and from that keeping a running check on whether the programme is liable to over-run, under-run or run to time.

Fixed items and buffers

Because we break a programme down into its component parts, we find that these fall into two distinct groupings:

(a) items of fixed duration;
(b) items of variable duration (buffers).

Fixed duration

The items of fixed duration are those that have been pre-recorded and edited. It might be possible to come out of one of these items early, but, generally speaking, the stories will either have to run their course while on air or be dropped from the programme altogether.

In the running order of our programme, we find a number of items of fixed duration:

1. Opening titles.
2. Stories on: Lost Children, New Technology, Soccer Violence, Housing Project, Lois Grey, Barn Murder, Hidden Treasure tease, War Crimes, State Visit, Hidden Treasure, Sport, Weather.
3. Closing titles.

If we abstract these from our running order we find that little remains except the links into and out of the items and the closing headlines.

The links into and out of the items are also fixed to a certain extent. Because VTR and telecine channels need a number of seconds in which to run up to speed, the PA cues the operators according to a word count based on the presenter's link into the item. If the links are altered after the script has been written they must:

(a) take into account the run-up time necessary into the pre-recorded item; and
(b) not give problems to the presenter who is reading his words from the tele-prompt.

But having said that, presenters often do have to ad lib for a few sentences in order to fill time or make cuts in order to save it.

Variable durations (buffers)

Items of variable duration, known as 'buffer items', give the producer leeway in adjusting the overall timing without having to resort to such drastic measures as dropping an entire item.

The buffer is always a 'live' item. It could be an interview, it could – as in our programme – be the closing headlines read by the presenter live in the studio; it could be a cake-making demonstration in a magazine-type programme. Whatever it is, its duration can be changed while on air, provided that the producer has been informed by the PA by how much the buffer is required to expand or contract.

Let us look at an example. A producer has estimated 3.00″ on a live interview, but just before we come to the interview the PA realises that the programme is over-running by 50″. The producer might then allot 2.10″ to the interview, thus checking the over-run and bringing the programme back to time.

The buffer item therefore is a means of getting the programme back to time if it is over- or under-running. However it often happens that the buffer itself will over- or under-run. The interview which was allotted only 2.10″ spreads to 2.24″, thus making our programme still over-running by 35″. So long as the producer is told, he or she can then decide whether to save time in another buffer item, drop a fixed item altogether or ask the PA to throw herself on the mercy of presentation to allow the over-run.

TITLE	EST. TIME	CUMULATIVE
1. TITLES (VTR)	0.10	
2. AMERICA REPORT (VTR)	1.30	1.40
3. REPORT FROM GREECE (Telecine)	2.00	3.40
4. " AUSTRALIA (Telecine)	.40	4.20
5. INTERVIEW	3.00?	7.20
6. AROUND THE WORLD (VTR)	1.10	8.30
7. STUDIO DISCUSSION	6.00?	14.30
8. CLOSING (VTR)	0.40	15.10

Example of timing. In this example, the items of variable duration, the buffers, are 5 and 7 (the interview and studio discussion). Everything else is pre-recorded and of fixed duration. When the real times for the pre-recorded items are known, the buffer durations can be altered to fit in with the overall running time of the programme. The essential time, in the above example, would be 14.30″, the end of the second buffer. It would be vital to hit that time correctly so that the closing credits, pre-recorded on VTR, could be shown in their entirety. If the programme has only a limited number of play-in machines there may be technical problems in changing the item at short notice if sufficient time is not allowed to reload the machine with the required item.

Time charts

So now we come to the sums. If you find it difficult to add and subtract time rapidly and accurately – and how often have PAs wished that time could be decimalized – you might find it helpful to block your numbers in groups of three or four.

TITLE	EST'D TIME		CUMULATIVE	ACTUAL TIME
1. TITLES	0.23 / 0.07	0 30		
2. LOST CHILDREN	0.15 / 2.20	2.35	3.05	2.05
3. NEW TECHNOLOGY	0.10 / 2.10	2.20	5.25	?
4. SOCCER VIOLENCE	0.15 / 1.00	1.15	6.40	1.45
5. SHORTS	0 40 / 1:10 / 0.55	2.45	9.25	
6. TEASE		0.15	9.40	0.15
7. WAR CRIMES	0.10 / 2.00	2.10	11.50	
8. STATE VISIT	0.20 / 1.05	1.25	13.15	2.05
9. HIDDEN TREASURE	0.15 / 1.40	1.55	15.10	1.55
10. SPORT	0.30 / 2.05	2.35	17.45	2.50
11. WEATHER	0.10 / 1.05	1.15	19.00	1.20
12. CLOSING		0.35	19.35	0.35
13. GOODNIGHT VTR	0.35 / 0.15	0.50	20.25	0.50

Example of a time chart. The two figures given for each sequence comprise (a) the duration of the link and (b) the duration of the pre-recorded insert. Together they make the third figure, the producer's estimated time.

It is far easier to add up

3.40	1.20	0.30
2.20	3.55	0.15
1.55	2.35	1.25
7.55	7.50	2.10

and then add together the three totals rather than be confronted by a long column of numbers. But, as with everything, you will get faster with practice.

Rounding up and down

Many PAs find it far easier to round up and down to multiples of five when working out timings. In the long run they find that the discrepancies will balance out.

But programmes of short duration, say five minutes or under, generally need the timing to be exact and for any programme where the timing has to be absolutely precise to the second, PAs will usually work with the exact figures.

Chart

On the example shown, the first column is for the producer's estimated timings. The duration for each sequence comprises the two elements shown: the link and the insert.

The second column shows the cumulative timings, adding up to a total overall running time of 20.25″.

As the actual times are known, they are written in column 3 and any changes noted in terms of the overall duration of the programme. In our programme, the first accurate duration given is for Sequence 10, which at 2.50″ is 15″ over the estimate.

Then we are given the timing for Sequence 6 which, at 15″ is the same as the estimate. Sequence 11 is 5″ over, making our programme at this stage 20″ over the estimated running time. But it is early yet and although the fact should be noted by the PA, the producer need not be informed.

When we get the timing for Sequence 4 we find that it is over its estimate by 30″ – bringing the overall spread up to 50″.

We hear that Sequence 3 will be late. It could become what is known as a 'floater', that is, fitted into the programme whenever it is completed. Its estimated duration must therefore be kept in mind if it is not ready when the programme goes on air.

Sequence 8 is now complete and its duration is 2.05″ – 40″ over the estimate, making the overall spread now 1.30″. You are about to inform the producer when you hear that Sequence 2 is only 2.05″, instead of the estimated 2.35″. The overall spread is now back to 1.00″.

Sequences 12 and 13 are as estimated, Sequence 9 we already know and at around this point you have assembled enough information to start back-timing.

Back and forward timing

You can now cumulatively forward time, back time or use a combination of both in order to see how the overall duration of the programme is working out.

Backtiming enables you to go on the air with the minimum of information. Because the aim is to get off the air smoothly and on time, in one sense the timings at the front of the programme are relatively less important than those at the end, and if you are in the situation of having only a few accurate durations when you go on the air, you cannot therefore work logically from Sequence 1 to Sequence 13 in order to find out how much over or under the programme is running. So you work backwards, knowing that you must go into the last fixed items of your programme at specific times.

For example, in our programme, the only buffer we have is the closing headlines, Sequence 12. We have therefore to go into Sequence 13 with the minimum of 15" for the closing titles which are on VTR. Then we ought to allow a decent time for the presenters to say goodnight. The producer estimated 35". So that on our overall running time of 20.25" we have to go into Sequence 13 at 19.35" or, at very worst, 20.10", so that the closing titles may be shown in full before the programme is taken off the air.

Buffer in the middle

If you have a buffer item of, say, an interview, somewhere in the middle of the programme, you might find it useful to backtime to the end of the interview and forward time to the start of the interview, which would then give you the duration of the interview item, which would be the time left between those two figures.

On an interview of an estimated duration of 4.00" the backtime figure comes out at, say, 14.30", that is, in timing backwards from the end of the programme. Forward timing from the start of the programme to the beginning of the interview brings us to 11.30", therefore either the interview can only be allowed to continue for 3.00" and not the estimated 4.00", or some other cuts will have to be made. That is the producer's responsibility.

Forward timing

If you have a programme which is in two distinct halves, the first half being a mixture of live and pre-recorded and the entire second half being a pre-recorded package of fixed duration, you would probably find that you would only forward time to the start of the second half of the programme.

Backtiming

Conversely, if the entire first half of your programme is pre-recorded and the second half a mixture, you would probably only backtime, as you would naturally come out of the first half of the programme at the set time.

Opting

If your programme has items from other studio centres being transmitted in different parts of the country, then the moment of opting in or out is critical and it is usual to forward time to the opt and back time to the end of the opt.

Commercial break

Again, if you have a commercial break at a fixed point within the programme, you might forward and back time to that point. But generally speaking, the commer-

TITLE	EST. TIME	CUM.	ACTUAL	BACKTIMING
1. TITLES	0.30			
2. LOST CHILDREN	2.35	3.05	2.05	
3. NEW TECHNOLOGY	2.20	5.25		
4. SOCCER VIOLENCE	1.15	6.40	1.45	
5. SHORTS	2.45	9.25		
6. TEASE	0.15	9.40	0.15	
7. WAR CRIMES	2.10	11.50		10,50
8. STATE VISIT	1.25	13.15	2.05	12,55
9. HIDDEN TREASURE	1.55	15.10	1.55	14.50
10. SPORT	2.35	17.45	2.50	17.40
11. WEATHER	1.15	19.00	1.20	19.00
12. CLOSING	0.35	19.35	0.35	19.35
13. GOODNIGHT/VTR	0.50	20.25	0.50	20.25

Example of backtiming. Backtiming is always cumulative, working backwards from the total running time of the programme. By comparing the estimated cumulative running time of 11.50″ at Sequence 7, by the backtiming figure of 10.50″ we find that the programme has spread by 1.00″.

cial breaks are variable to a certain extent and liaison with presentation would take place about their positioning in the programme.

Lack of time!

It is of course very easy to imagine a fictitious programme and work through the different stages. As any PA who has worked on live programmes knows only too well, the luxury of being able to complete time charts and work out, before going on air, the many sums necessary, are minimal, and the likelihood of the running order being adhered to is likewise equally minimal.

Writing on script

Some PAs do not use their running order or time chart when they go into studio, but transfer all their timings on to the script. They do this because it is simpler in the studio to look at just one piece of paper, i.e. the script, rather than two or three. They also do it because if, for some reason, the running order is changed on air then it becomes complicated working from something that is out of date and they find it simpler to shuffle the pages of script around. These PAs will work on their running order until just before they go into the gallery, then transfer their timings and work solely from the script.

Other PAs will work from the running order or time charts because they can see the timings making up the programme in its entirety, and on national news PAs find that there is no point even having a script as there would not be time to read it.

Digital countdown clock

If you are fortunate enough to have a digital countdown clock available, you might include another column on your time chart, backtiming from zero, but that is only if you are certain that the running time of the programme is fixed and will not be changed on air. Then you will know, for example, that at the start of Sequence 11 your countdown clock should read 2.45″ to the end of the programme.

The news script

The script on a live news-type programme is different from most other kinds of scripts in that it forms the *basis* of a working document: it is not a finished document in itself and it is not a complete record of the programme.

You would not, in fifty years time, be able to pick up a script from a news programme of today and, solely by reading it, re-live the programme in its entirety. All you would be able to do is read the links between items and gain a sketchy idea about the intervening stories with, perhaps, their overall duration and 'out' words.

The real meat of the programme, the news items themselves, are not written in the script. This is because of the immediacy of news stories. The items would only just have been edited for transmission and there would certainly have been no time and no occasion for a transcript to be made. And of course any elements such as live interviews could not be scripted in advance.

So the script is a mixture of accurately scripted links, exactly as the presenter will read them – unless the presenter is given to unscripted ad libs – scripted voice-over (V/O) commentary to be read over specific news stories and as much information about the pre-recorded items as exist at the time the script is typed.

Stand-by warnings might be typed in as reminders and possibly cues to roll in the various pre-recorded items from their different sources. But many PAs prefer to mark up their own scripts with these cues.

When is it typed?

If the newsroom is computerized the scripts will be typed by the reporters themselves. Printed copies will be run off when the links have been checked by the producer and presenter.

If there is no computer, the script has to be typed by the PA or a typist as and when the links are drafted. So the script will not be typed in chronological order and it might well be that parts of it are still in the typing and distribution stages when the programme has gone on the air. On many programmes of this nature, the finished pages are never finally stapled together.

```
                         SEQUENCE 9 : HIDDEN TREASURE

   /S/B TC/



   CAM 2                        /Hidden treasure.  The very thought
   ANDREW IN VISION
                                of it conjures up visions of gold

                                coins, silver tankards, the rich and

                                precious heritage of days long past.

                                But hidden treasure can be of a very

                                different kind as Mrs Mary Watkins

                                found when she sent off a parcel of

                                old clothes to the Red Cross in

                                response to the latest aid appeal.
   TELECINE                     Chris Johns reports:/
   HIDDEN TREASURE


   CAP : MARY WATKINS           DUR: 1'35"

   at   ..........
                                Out words:  "..go rummaging in your attics."


   CAMS 2 & 3                   /Sport link next/
   ANDREW + CAP
```

Example of a page of script.

Page numbers

Because it is typed in this way, consecutive page numbering becomes meaningless and each section is referred to, both in and out of the studio, by its item or sequence number, each sequence comprising the individual news story plus its link.

Each sequence must therefore start on a fresh page and the only numbering that usually occurs is when more than one page relates to the same sequence.

Layout

The standard layout for camera scripts is one where the picture details are placed on the lefthand side of the page and the dialogue on the right. The pages are typed single side only and camera scripts are usually duplicated or photocopied on yellow paper.

It is extremely important to allow plenty of space when typing the script as the vision mixer, director and PA will all be marking up their copies and plenty of room is appreciated.

Lefthand side

The visuals are usually typed on the lefthand side of the page in capital letters and the line across the page denotes a cut by the vision mixer to another shot whether it be to another camera's output or to another source, i.e. VTR, telecine, etc.

Above the line the camera or source is marked and below the line an indication is given of the picture.

Standby warnings and instructions are also marked on the lefthand side of the page, usually framed in boxes so that they stand out.

The duration of the pre-recorded item is typed in, if this is known, together with the 'out' words.

Righthand side

The presenter's links are typed out in full in double spacing on the righthand side of the page. These are identical to the words seen by the presenter in the studio and read by him or her from the teleprompt. If any changes are made, the PA must note them on her own script as they might affect the cueing in of different sources.

If the example on page 33 is studied it will be clear that this type of script does not contain a great deal of information. Apart from the links, the information given is patchy and the little contained is, needless to say, subject to change and alteration.

Providing the PA is working on a programme where she is expected to give standby warnings and roll in pre-recordings, as soon as she receives any part of the script she begins marking it up.

Marking up a script

Some PAs write very little down on their scripts, keeping most of the information in their heads and trusting in their memories and their ability to make instant calculations from a glance at their stopwatch. They work in this way firstly because there might well not be time to do anything else, secondly because once something is written down it tends to become fixed and rigid and difficult to change when changes occur, thirdly because it is time-consuming to keep writing and fourthly because constant alterations will make the script messy and unreadable.

At the other end of the scale is the PA who trusts nothing to her memory, least of all numbers on a stopwatch. Everything will be written down, probably in red pen – all the standbys, all the countdowns, everything.

Most PAs fall somewhere in the middle, probably marking up their scripts as much as possible in the time given, possibly using pencil to start with and only using a red pen in the studio.

Roll cues

If the PA is expected to roll the various sources then, whatever else she marks or leaves off her script, she should note the cue to roll.

The operator of the VTR, ENG or telecine channel will have been alerted by the PA's standby warning and will be waiting, finger poised on the button, for the command to 'Roll!' (or 'Run!' depending upon which term is in common use by the company).

All machines take a certain time to lace up and reach the correct running speed. Even the ACR (Automatic Cartridge Recorder), which has an instant start requires up to a second to allow for the operator's reaction time. The times vary according to machine and company. For example, some VTR machines need a 10" run-up time and some only 5".

Throughout this book I have used a 5" run-up time for VTR and ENG and an 8" run-up time for telecine (TC).

Marking the cue

If the presenter's link allows sufficient time, you can mark the script on a word cue. It is standard practice to count three words to a second when working out cues. Therefore when marking up a script for a 5" roll, you should count back fifteen words in the preceding link. For an 8" roll, you count back twenty-four words. The speed of delivery might vary from presenter to presenter and you might have to adjust your word cue accordingly, but the difference will be minimal and it is safe to consider three words to a second as the norm.

Ring the precise word, as shown in the example on page 36, and write the cue in large letters – perhaps in pencil to begin with and then confirmed in red pen if you have the chance of a rehearsal and are certain that the cue is correct.

Time cue

If you are rolling in one source after another in quick succession or have insufficient time in the link to use a word cue, you will need to calculate the time at which you need to roll the second and subsequent sources and mark them on your script.

For example, your first roll into a VTR item is off a word cue. This item is 30" long. There is no link into the second item which is on film and lasts 15" and from the film you are straight into the third item on VTR lasting 55".

You would mark your script first to give a word cue into the first item. Then you would mark down that at 22" into the VTR item you would roll the film item (i.e. 8" run-up time for the telecine channel) and at 10" into the film item you would roll the third story which is on VTR.

Channel number

If you know the number of the source channel, assuming that there is more than one, mark that on the script.

One company, using a large number of channels, identifies each one by the story title, therefore the cue would be 'Roll VTR – Lost Children', rather than 'Roll VTR – 12'.

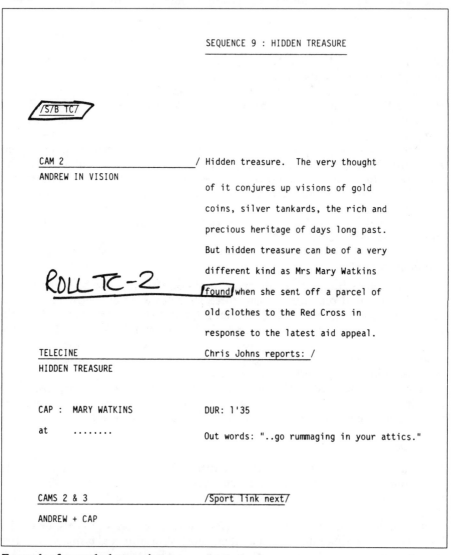

```
                              SEQUENCE 9 : HIDDEN TREASURE
                              ─────────────────────────────


    /S/B  TC/



  CAM 2                        / Hidden treasure.  The very thought
  ANDREW IN VISION
                               of it conjures up visions of gold

                               coins, silver tankards, the rich and

                               precious heritage of days long past.

                               But hidden treasure can be of a very

    ROLL TC-2                  different kind as Mrs Mary Watkins

                               [found] when she sent off a parcel of

                               old clothes to the Red Cross in

                               response to the latest aid appeal.
  TELECINE                     Chris Johns reports: /
  HIDDEN TREASURE


  CAP :  MARY WATKINS          DUR: 1'35

  at    ........
                               Out words: "..go rummaging in your attics."



  CAMS 2 & 3                   /Sport link next/
  ANDREW + CAP
```

Example of a marked up script.

Some or all of the following can be marked on the script, firstly if there is time, secondly if the information is available and thirdly, and most important, if the PA finds it helpful.

Standbys

Standbys are reminders to the PA to give warnings to different people at different times in the course of the programme. Operators of VTR, telecine, caption generators, music or tape inserts, presenters, camera operators, anyone in fact directly involved with the programme might need to receive a warning standby from the studio gallery.

Capgens

If name superimpositions are cued in by the PA then they should be marked on the script, provided they are not given the information on a separate source sheet.

Countdowns

Some PAs like to write down the countdown timings for each separate item.

In a VTR insert, for example, with an overall duration of 1.25″, you would write the following countdowns:

at 25″	1.00″ left on VTR
at 55″	30″ left on VTR
at 1.10″	15″ left on VTR
at 1.15″	10″ left on VTR
at 1.20″	05″ counting out

But there is rarely time on a live news-type programme to work out and write down these figures in advance and there is the danger that, by doing so, the PA will never learn to read her stopwatch quickly and therefore never gain real expertise in live galleries. There is also the tendency, if the numbers are written on the script, of working too closely from the script and not watching the preview monitors.

But if, by writing everything down, it gives the PA the confidence and security to cope with the pressures of the studio at least in the early stages, then the method has its uses.

Counting in and out of programmes

Because of the complexity of many opening title sequences, PAs will usually find that they have to write down the countdowns into the programme involving, as they frequently do, a number of sources to be rolled almost simultaneously (back to back rolls), insert rolls, capgen counts and maybe grams as well.

And when coming off air, all PAs will be meticulous in counting out of the programme and will almost certainly work out and mark up the figures on their scripts, often backtiming from the real, i.e. the 'off air' time.

Source sheets

On some programmes a source sheet is filled in by the editors working on the different news items. Each item has its separate sheet and on it is given the story title, sequence number, channel from which it is to be generated, sound details, capgen details, the 'out' words and overall duration.

Any specific notes helpful to the director and PA are written in by the editor.

The source sheets should be filed in between the pages of the script as they arrive and are handed to the gallery PA.

SEQUENCE 1 : TITLES

/S/B VTR/ENG/

VTR 1   /
TITLES

-5" ROLL VTR-1
+7" " ENG-3
+11" " ENG-1
+14" - VTR-10
+17" - VTR-6

AT 12" WIPE TO FIRST HEADLINES
VISUAL

ENG 3   /   Q CHERRY (V/O)
DEVASTATED HOME + FAMILY

A family grieves in the aftermath of
today's horrific bomb blast..

ENG 1   /
HOSPITAL

Q ANDREW (V/O)

A new breakthrough in the fight against
cancer..

VTR 10   /
RACE COURSE

Q CHERRY (V/O)

The signs are bright for tomorrow's
big race..

VTR 6   /
ELEPHANT AT ZOO

Q ANDREW (V/O)

And Nelly the elephant has a good
night's rest.

CAM   /LINK TO BOMB BLAST NEXT/
CHERRY IN VISION

Example of a marked script with complex opening sequence.

SEQUENCE: 9

STORY: RAILWAYS

CHANNEL: VTR-6
(if known)

SOUND (v/o times etc.)	CAPGEN (Time and name)	ANY OTHER DETAILS
S.O.VT	@ 16" 'MICHAEL WRIGHT' @ 42" 'ALAN ROWSE'	HOLD ON LAST SHOT UNTIL TRAIN ENTERS TUNNEL (at 1'35")

DURATION: 1'35"

"OUT" WORDS: ".. there is no going back" (See above)

Example of a source sheet.

The 'live' studio: just before transmission

You have now reached the point where it is time to go to the studio. At this stage you will probably have some, if not all, of the script, together with source sheets for the items that have been edited. Your time chart will be as ready as is possible and you may, or may not, have begun backtiming.

What to take with you

Surprisingly little. Surprising because, generally speaking, it is the PA's lot to go from place to place burdened like a packhorse, but not in this instance. What you will need is the following:

Stopwatches

Unless you follow the practice of some PAs and only use one watch, you should take as many as you can find that are in working order.

Running order/time chart

Not a fresh one, but the one that you have been working on. It will contain the estimated timings, the real timings, where known, the cumulative timings and perhaps the start of backtiming.

Script

If the pages of script have been stapled together, you should separate them in order to slip in the *source sheets* at the relevant points. If you have a source sheet for a particular item and do not have the linking pages of script, keep the sheet to one side and you will then have a check on what is still missing from the script.

Coloured pens/pencils/eraser

Blank paper

And perhaps some mints or soothing sweets for when the pressure is on, together with - for the same reason - your own and the director's own favourite cuddly toy!

Personnel

Thus armed, you take your seat at the control desk of the studio gallery at the side of the director. On your other side will, in all probability, sit the producer of the day, unless he or she is pacing up and down at the back.

Also at the desk will be the vision mixer - unless the director performs that operation for himself - possibly an effects operator, the capgen operator and the studio supervisor (known in some companies as the technical manager).

On one side of the central control room is the sound control area and the lighting control area is on the other.

Equipment

In front of you is the desk containing a number of keys and buttons, telephones, a microphone on a stalk, possibly an inset stopwatch or the real time displayed dig-

'... together with – for the same reason – your own and the director's own favourite cuddly toy!'

itally and maybe a digital countdown clock.

Directly in front of the desk is a row of monitors of different sizes, the smaller ones showing the output of each individual source, one showing teleprompt, one for special effects, another for capgen, one turned to whatever programme is being currently transmitted and larger preview and transmission monitors.

Above that is the studio clock, hopefully in a clear position.

Talkback

Communication between the gallery and the studio floor is by means of a talkback system which is not picked up by the studio microphones.

Script check

The director may well take the studio through a script check, running rapidly over each link and each item, talking to the camera operators about what is required and ironing out any problems.

Rehearsal

If there is time, there may well be a rehearsal of one or two potentially difficult bits, for example, links into items that need precise timing, complex shots using electronic effects etc. These rehearsals would give the PA the chance to adjust roll cues if necessary.

PA responsibilities

During this run up to transmission, the PA will be fully occupied with a variety of different jobs. In no particular order these could include:

☐ receiving further pages of script and source sheets, putting them in sequence order, marking up the fresh script pages with roll cues and standbys;
☐ on receiving the source sheets with the – hopefully – correct durations of the insert items, the PA will note down the accurate timings on her chart, adjust the cumulative times accordingly and keep up to date with the overall duration of the programme;
☐ liaising with the producer on the question of overall duration, noting any changes and informing the director and studio;
☐ checking that her talkback is operating, making contact with the operators of the VTR, ENG and telecine channels and running through the order of items with them, checking the identity of the source channel for each item;
☐ checking that her stopwatches are working properly and finding out from the studio supervisor whether the studio clock is running to correct time;
☐ making contact with presentation and liaising concerning the times in and out of the programme together with times for commercial breaks should these occur;
☐ making contact with other studio centres or outside broadcast units for live injects into the programme;
☐ if the overall time as given by presentation differs from the original running time, the PA will adjust her timings accordingly and inform the producer and director;
☐ the PA will check the order for capgens;
☐ if the PA has a digital countdown watch she will pre-set it to the exact running time of the programme;
☐ if the telephone rings either the PA or the studio supervisor will answer it;

and, in addition to all the above, the PA *must* at all times keep an ear open for the director, count in and out of items being rehearsed and make changes to the script and time chart where necessary.

Five minutes to transmission

The PA should give minute warnings to the studio from about five minutes prior to transmission. Certainly a one minute warning must be given followed by fifteen second countdowns.

'During this run up to transmission, the PA will be fully occupied with a variety of different jobs.'

Standbys should be given for the channels needed for the opening sequence, the digital countdown clock started and the programme counted on the air from – 10″.

The opening titles should be rolled and at zero the overall and insert watches started.

Different systems

There are a number of different systems in use for running a live programme, dependent upon custom and the complexity of the programme.

In a straight news programme, with its great number of items, its liability for very last minute changes while on air, its need for absolute split-second precision in timing, it may be that the PA is unable to do anything during the transmission other than overall timing and countdowns. The director would give the standbys and roll and cue the sources.

On some live programmes the complexity of the content would require two PAs to be in the gallery, one to time and give countdowns, the other to roll and cue. But many live programmes rely on just one PA who is responsible for all these elements. Very often, in that situation, the director does his own vision mixing. We will assume, in this section of the book, that there is just one PA in the gallery.

A question of priorities

If we break down the PA's job in a live gallery into its component parts we find an order begins to emerge. Some things are of greater importance than others.

Timing

It is of over-riding importance to get on and off the air smoothly and cleanly. Everything else is subservient to that first priority although from it naturally flow things like good liaison with the producer and rolling into and counting out of insert items correctly.

Previewing

All PAs, whatever type of programme they work on, must watch the preview monitor for the shot that is to be transmitted next.

Rolling and counting

Having ensured that the beginning and end of the programme are correct, the PA's next priority is to make the body of the programme go as smoothly as possible by rolling in the insert items at the correct times and counting in and out of items.

Standbys and cueing

It is important to give warning standbys, but it does not head your list of priorities, neither does cueing in capgens. If necessary, they must be dropped in favour of more vital work.

3

Learn to love your stopwatch

A PA without a stopwatch is like a fish out of water. Your watch is part of you, you should feel naked without it. It is the core and the essence of the live PA's job.

To know your stopwatch requires far more than the mere ability to stop it, start it and flick it back to zero. You have to be able to read it, not just in the sense of being able to tell the time quickly and accurately, but to be able to work out instant calculations from the information it gives.

Some PAs find it helpful to think of the face of the stopwatch as an orange which they divide into segments: first quarter, second quarter and so on. It might sound fanciful but if you are giving countdowns through a pre-recorded item you should be able to glance at your watch and know that in an overall duration of 55″, when the second hand has reached 25″ there will be 30″ left on the insert, and if thinking of the face of the watch as an orange or apple or football helps, then you should think of it as such.

Analogue and digital

This is where a stopwatch with an analogue face has the advantage over a digital watch. A digital watch will only show you the time it is now, whereas with an analogue watch you see the time in relation to what is past and what is to come.

Therefore in giving countdowns out of an insert you are not just keeping a lot of abstract numbers in your head, you are looking at the 30″, the 15″ and so on as a shape, a shape on the round face of the dial from the position of the second hand and in relation to the overall duration of the insert. Back to the orange in fact!

That is not to say that time shown in digits is of no use. It is, especially in a digital countdown clock which can be pre-set with the programme's running time.

Digital countdown clock

If the running time is 18.32″ then you can pre-set those figures and, by starting the clock as you go on air it will count down to zero.

As you will be extraordinarily busy with other things at the precise moment you go on air you might like to pre-set your countdown clock a minute or two early – setting it for the programme running time plus one or two.

The advantage of a digital countdown clock is that at any point you, or anyone else, can see exactly how long remains to the end of the programme. It is a useful back-up in situations where things have gone wrong and you no longer have any idea of the overall timing, and you can use it to advantage to get you off the air, but do not rely on it exclusively, firstly because it can and sometimes does go wrong and secondly because only certain companies provide the facility.

These clocks can also count up from zero or from any pre-set time and therefore can be used as normal stopwatches.

Number of stopwatches

It might have seemed rather excessive when I stated that you should take a number of stopwatches to the gallery but watches have been known to break down and to PAs whose master overall watch has unaccountably stopped in the middle of a live transmission – and it has happened to a surprising amount of PAs – a back-up master then becomes essential.

At the beginning of the programme you start one or two master overall watches and put them some way out of reach so that you are not tempted by their proximity to confuse them with an insert watch and zero them by mistake – and that has been known to happen before now!

If you feel that you might in any way be confused by the plethora of stopwatches spread before you, you could always mark the glass of the master watch with a red pen.

Using just one watch

On some news programmes the PAs work solely from just one stopwatch. They do this because it is less time-wasting than going from one watch to another and because there is less risk of confusion.

They work off one watch by noting down on their running order the overall time *as they go into* a pre-recorded item. They then add to this figure the duration of the item and the cumulative figure they reach gives them the basis for working out countdowns to the end of the item.

For example, if the time on going into the item is 12.30″ on the overall watch and the duration of the item is 1.20″, then the 'out' time of the item will be 13.50″. You can then give countdowns based on that time: 30″ countdown at 13.20″; 15″ countdown at 13.35″ and so on.

This system has the advantage of being able to give accurate overall timings at the *start* of each item, rather than at the end. It means that you have only one watch to worry about, rather than several. However, it is not easy to master the technique and does rely on a lot of timings being written down, which presupposes that the PA is solely concerned with durations and does not roll and cue as well.

Real time versus stopwatch time

PAs on some programmes work not from a master overall stopwatch, building up the running time of the programme from zero, but from the real time as shown by the studio or digital clock in front of the PA. They argue, very validly, that because the programme is live, it is the real time that matters, i.e. getting off the air at 18.32.35.

On their running order or time chart, therefore, these PAs will add up their cumulative times in the context of the real time and backtime from the real off-air time.

The advantage of this system is that the studio clock and their own timings match and their backtimings for getting off the air will be correspondingly simpler.

The disadvantages to this system are:

(a) if the running time of the programme is always the same but the on-air time varies and is not known until just prior to transmission, the PA would not have been able to work out backtimings in advance;

Learn to love your stopwatch.

(b) if the running time of the programme is subject to last minute changes the PA would have to re-do quite complex sums as it is harder to work in large figures than in small – sums involving six digits seem more daunting than those with four.

If the PA is working off real time, however, it is essential that she either has a digital clock in front of her on the desk or the studio clock is clearly positioned for her use.

Counting down from 10"

But having so far stressed the importance of learning to read your stopwatch at a glance, you should make it your business to learn how to count down from 10" without reference to one. It will make you less dependent upon your watch and more able to preview the monitors at critical moments.

Timing on air

Overall timing

How does the PA keep a running total of the overall timings amid the welter of rolling, cueing, counting in and out and all the other sundry duties undertaken while on air?

At the end of each sequence you should note down the cumulative time which you will get from your master stopwatch – unless you are using just one watch. You note this down either in an additional column on your running order or time chart, or on your script if you work solely from that.

By comparing this figure with your estimated cumulative timing you will be able to work out, at the end of each sequence, whether the programme is running to time, under or over. You inform the producer and he or she will then make the necessary adjustments to enable the programme to come out on time.

Producer's options

There are a number of options open to the producer:

(a) the buffer item can be lengthened or shortened;
(b) if the programme is under-running, the presenter could be asked to ad lib for a few seconds, or a standby item could be inserted;
(c) if the programme is over-length then some lines could be cut from the presenter or a sequence dropped altogether;
(d) presentation could be contacted and permission sought for an over-run of the allotted time.

What is essential, however, is that the producer is given the information by the PA, and given it with enough time for the options to be considered and carried out.

When do you note down the timing?

If you find that at the end of each sequence you are too busy to glance at your overall watch and write down the result, you might find that you get into a system of glancing at your master watch at, say, one minute to the end of the insert when you have slightly more leisure. You could write down the figure, adding on one minute, at that point, thus leaving you clear to count out of the item.

Ending the programme

All these timings are of course carrying you inexorably closer to the end of the programme and as it progresses you will know by how much or how little the programme running time has changed. If you look at the time chart below you will see that by the time we reach the end of sequence 7 we are 10″ over-running. That is not serious and the producer would probably make the decision to cut 10″ from Sequence 17, the closing headlines.

	Est'd	Cum	Actual	Backtiming	On air
1. IDENT/TITLES	0.30	0.30	0.30		0.30
2. LOST CHILDREN	2.35	3.05	2.05		2.35
3. NEW TECHNOLOGY	2.20	5.25	2.05		4.40
4. SOCCER VIOLENCE	1.15	6.40	1.45		6.25
5. SHORTS	2.45	9.25	2.15		8.40
6. TEASE	0.15	9.40	0.15		8.55
7. WAR CRIMES	2.10	11.50	2.05	10.50	11.00
8. STATE VISIT	1.25	13.15	20.05	12.55	
9. HIDDEN TREASURE	1.55	15.10	1.55	14.50	
10. SPORT	2.35	17.45	2.50	17.40	
11. WEATHER	1.15	19.00	1.20	19.00	
12. CLOSING	0.35	19.35	0.35	19.35	
13. FINALLY/VTR	0.50	20.25	0.50	20.25	

Example of a time chart.

We could then work out the end of the programme precisely by backtiming from the 'off air' time (see the far column on the time chart). Whatever happens, at 20.10″ we *must* go into the closing titles which are of 15″ duration and recorded on VTR. That means that at 20.05″ *precisely* (allowing for the 5″ run up time for the VTR machine) we must roll VTR.

Boxes

On the final page of the script we would work out a box of final timings, something like the example below, although probably not as detailed:

at 19.25″   Standby VTR/1.00″ to end programme
at 19.55″   '15″ left' warning to presenter
at 20.00″   '10″ left' warning to presenter
at 20.05″   'Roll VTR' (perhaps linked to a word cue, perhaps rolled on time alone if the presenter is ad libbing the closing words)
             '5″ left' countdown for presenter
at 20.10″   'On VTR for 15″' warning
at 20.15″   10″ countdown to end of programme
at 20.25″   Off air

Coming to the end of a live transmission depends very much on the composition of the last couple of sequences of the programme, but the countdown timings to coming off air are, for safety's sake, better worked out and written down as there might be a lot of things to say and timings to give and it is vital that nothing is left out.

One minute clock

Because the last minute of live transmission is crucial, some presenters like to have a clock started in the studio at one minute to the end of the programme in order for them to time their closing links precisely.

This clock might be set by the PA from the gallery or by the floor manager in the studio on instructions from the PA. The PA herself might wish to start a stopwatch at one minute to the end of transmission – unless she has a digital countdown clock which serves the same purpose – and she could then take her end timings from the insert watch rather than the master overall one.

If she has been working throughout the programme from a master stopwatch, she might like to use real time to get off the air and work out her final box based on real time.

Closing credits

There might well be closing credits that would have to be cued in from the capgen machine at fixed times. These would be added to the box.

Pre-fading music

If there is closing music on tape or disc, this usually has to be prefaded on a cue from the PA. Let us say for example that the quarter-inch tape containing the music runs at an overall duration of 40″, while the duration of the closing credits is 30″. We therefore have 10″ of unwanted music.

SEQUENCE 13

/S/B VTR/   /S/B PREFADE/

CAM 1   /   CHERRY
CHERRY IN VISION
                                         And finally, a happy story

                                         from Loudwater Zoo. Two weeks

                                         ago, Henry the elephant lay

                                         down in his cage, spurned all

                                         food and grew progressively

                                         weaker. After trying every   Q PREFADE

                                         possible remedy, John Tombs,   GRAMS AT

                                         his keeper, finally advertised   19.45

                                         for a mate for Henry. Now, two
ROLL VTR-1
                                         days (after) the arrival of Nelly,

                                         Henry has taken on a new lease

CAM 2   of life. Goodnight. /
2-s CHERRY AND ANDREW

VTR—1   /   19.55
HENRY & NELLY AT ZOO   /F/UP GRAMS/

                                         CLOSING CREDITS

DUR: 40" available   Presented by
                                         Cherry Stone   and Andrew Plum
CAPGENS

                                         Producer

                                                                  30"

                                                                  20.25

Example of pre-fading music. On a script, sound details are always written on the far right hand side of the page. During rehearsal, confirm with the Grams Operator the length of the closing music, and ask him to set up the grams for your pre-fade. On many live programmes the Grams Op will pre-fade the closing music on his own timings. It is therefore most important to tell him of any alteration to the running time.

Clearly the end of the music must coincide with the end of the programme. Therefore the PA would calculate 40″ back from the programme end, i.e. at 19.45″ (in our programme of 20.25″) and would cue the music to start at that point. However, because the first 10″ are not required, the cue would be to 'pre-fade' the music at 19.45″ and another cue to 'fade-up' the music would be made 10″ later, i.e. at 19.55″. The music would then end with the end of the programme.

Keep your head up! The importance of previewing

Having started my broadcasting career in radio, not television, I was used when recording a radio show to keeping my eyes firmly fixed on my stopwatch and script on the desk in front of me. There was no point or necessity for me to watch the performers in the studio grouped, as they were, around a microphone.

When I began work in television I found it extremely difficult to tear my eyes away from the script and stopwatch in order to look up at the monitors. There was, I think, an innate fear that by raising my head I would lose my place in my script, be unable to read my stopwatch and lose any grip on the programme.

I know that I am not alone in that fear even among PAs who did not start, as I did, in radio. There are many PAs who find it very hard to look up from their watches and scripts. It is, in one sense, a striving after security. The script is simple enough to relate to and understand; the stopwatch likewise. But the moment you start watching the many different monitors there is the danger of becoming confused.

On any television programme however it is essential to watch the preview monitor for the shot that is to be transmitted next. On a live programme it is vital for the following reasons:

Watching the ident

When giving a standby warning for an insert item, you should always check that the correct insert is ready on the correct channel. There will be a visual ident on an item on VTR in the form of a clock and the title of the piece. There may be a visual ident on ENG but not always and an item on film will have no ident at the front, just a film leader which is a series of numbers representing either seconds or feet. If there is no visual ident you should always check with the operator that the correct item is laced up.

It is not enough to assume that the right stories will automatically be ready. In nine times out of ten they will be, but the make-up, as it is called, of which items go to which channels can sometimes be very complicated and mistakes can happen especially if one or more of the stories arrive late or the running order changes at the last minute. You are the last check before transmission that the correct item will follow the presenter's link.

Counting in from the ident

You should always count into the insert from the ident clock or the film leader, while watching the monitor, and not from your watch. You should start your insert watch from the moment zero is reached. This will give you an accurate timing for the item.

Counting out of insert

You will look a complete fool and be responsible for confusing the entire studio if you count out of an item without watching the monitor. You might have been given a wrong duration or the director might decide to come out of the insert item early and there you would be, your eyes glued to your stopwatch, counting out of an item that possibly finished five seconds ago, or that continues long after you have supposedly counted it out. In addition, if you are counting out of an item that has already finished, your overall timing will be inaccurate.

'And it has happened!'

Do beware of the pre-recorded item that contains shots of the presenter in the studio. It is very easy to panic and think that you are out of the recording and live in the studio.

The ultimate in counting out would be to count out of the entire programme oblivious of the fact that it came off the air ten seconds ago. And it has happened!

Cueing in capgens

On your source sheet you have made a note to cue in the capgen of Mrs Joan Bloggs, Chairman of the Blogsworth District Council at 1.25″ into the item. At 1.20″ into the item therefore you count in to the capgen, 'five . . . four . . . three . . . two . . . one . . .', and the capgen reading 'Mrs Joan Bloggs, Chairman, Blogsworth District Council' is superimposed not over a shot of the honourable lady but over a shot of a large pig! Neither you nor the vision mixer were watching the monitor.

To sum up, therefore, your job is not just to read off figures from a stopwatch and do sums in a mindless, unthinking way, but to be intelligently involved with the content of the programme.

Previewing is very hard for a number of PAs, especially those involved with live programmes where the stopwatch can become an obsession. But it is essential. And for those people who say that it is just not possible to keep an intelligent eye on the monitors while working from the script and stopwatches, the answer must be to practise and work out for yourselves how best you can accommodate these things. You will probably find that there are occasions when you will hold your script up on a level with the monitors so that your eyes can flick quickly from one to the other. (This is particularly useful in fast shot calling sequences which are described in Chapter 8).

Rolling, cueing and counting

Insert items

The instruction to the operator to start the machine containing the pre-recorded insert is sometimes given by the director, but more usually by the PA.

1. Standby warning

First of all a standby warning is given at anything from thirty seconds to a minute before the item is to be transmitted. The videotape or film channel operator will respond by a 'beep' to show that he or she has taken heed of the warning. If there is no response to the standby, the PA *must* repeat it with more urgency.

2. Ident clock/film leader

The ident clock (if VTR or ENG) should appear on one of the monitors. The PA should check that the correct story title is shown. If the item is on film, a leader will appear on the monitor and a number will be displayed.

3. Run-up time

Each machine needs a certain time in order to run up to speed. These times vary and the PA will have worked out, on the basis of the run-up time needed, when to give the command for the machine to be started. This can be worked out:

(a) On a word cue. Counting back three words to a second from the end of the presenter's link into the item will give the precise word on which the PA gives the command to the operator. (In some companies the PA has control of starting the machine herself.) This can be adjusted in rehearsal if the presenter speaks faster or slower.

(b) On a time cue. If the presenter's link does not contain sufficient words to allow a word cue, or if the inserts are rolled back to back (one insert leading straight into another insert), or if there are inserts within the pre-recorded item, then the PA has to work out time cues for the command.

(c) On an action cue, e.g. lighting a cigarette, sitting down, or whatever has been worked out in advance between the presenter and PA. This would occur in situations where there is no precise timing in the live section before the pre-recorded insert and no scripted link.

'If there is no response to the standby, the PA *must* repeat it with more urgency.'

4. Command

Different companies use different command words and the order in which they use them varies. Everyone, understandably, defends the system they are used to and clearly one must give the recognized and explicit form of command that is common at the time.

5. Counting through insert

The PA will count through the insert, cue in capgens as necessary and count out, giving the last word or two of dialogue.

Cueing presenters

The director, in general, cues the presenters, however the PA usually cues them when they have live out-of-vision dialogue to speak over a pre-recorded insert.

Cue dots

These are visual warning marks, in the form of small squares in one corner of the television screen which appear and disappear during the last minute or thirty seconds of a programme or leading to an opt or commercial break.

Cue dots are for the use of presentation or the PA in a live gallery, who will be watching for the cue dot of the preceding programme in order to count her own programme on the air.

It is sometimes the responsibility of the PA to put the cue dot on at approximately one minute before the commercial break and take it out at − 5″.

Just keep counting

Counting is a major function of the PA throughout a live transmission. She will:

☐ count down into the programme
☐ count into, through and out of every pre-recorded item
☐ count capgens on to the air
☐ count presenters into live voice-overs, into, through and out of interviews
☐ count out of the programme.

Counting into the programme

The PA should keep the studio informed at regular intervals before they go on air. It is usual to give at least a five minute warning, then warnings every minute. From one minute to transmission she will give 15″ counts and count down from 10″ into the programme.

Inserts

The PA should count into the pre-recorded inserts, counting down the number of seconds remaining on the VTR clock or film leader.

Once into the pre-recorded item, the PA should give the total duration of the insert, i.e. 'Three minutes on VTR, three minutes', then warnings every minute, 'Two minutes left on VTR, two minutes'. From one minute she should give 15″ counts and count out of the insert and back to the studio from 5″.

Capgens

If the PA knows that there is a capgen at 1.30″ into the insert, she should give a 5″ countdown to the superimposition and, if required, count through the 5″ or so that the director wants it held on the screen.

Presenters

During an interview, the PA should give the presenter counts to the end, either directly or via the floor manager. Some presenters like to be counted out of interviews and some do not. The PA should find out in advance what system the presenter prefers.

Commercial breaks

These would be treated by the PA as if they were insert items. Presentation would inform the gallery how long the break was to be and the PA would count to the break, start an insert watch for the duration of the break and count back to the studio at the end.

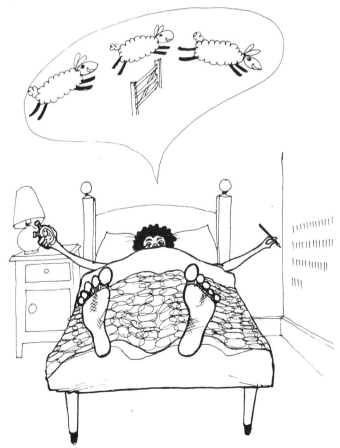

Just keep counting.

Counting out of programme

The count out of the programme is usually complicated and requires a list or box of timings worked out in advance to enable the PA to get off the air smoothly. She would certainly give a 'one minute to end of programme' warning and then 15" warnings until counting out from 10".

Is anyone listening out there?

It is possible to feel very isolated in the gallery, despite being surrounded by people and knowing that when you speak you are communicating with many others. Despite that it is possible for you to sit at the control desk, counting in and counting out and a small corner of your brain would be wondering, just what is the point of it all? Is anyone listening out there? If you stopped counting, surely the programme would continue, unchecked, except for a blessed silence?

Yes, it most probably would continue, but you would throw everyone into a good deal of confusion. For they rely on the PA to guide them through the programme, to keep them informed about what is happening at that moment, what is to happen next and how long they have, in terms of time, at every stage of the programme.

Studio discussions and interviews

Studio-based discussions and interviews take up an increasingly large amount of television. Such programmes are usually transmitted live or recorded 'as live' with the minimum of post production work.

An interview can range from a simple injection into an otherwise news-oriented programme when a political figure or 'expert in the field' is asked to comment on a news item, to a whole programme structured around a person-to-person talk of the 'chat show' variety. Then there are programmes involving discussions between groups of people. These frequently include the studio audience.

Whatever the situation, because these discussions or interviews are more or less unscripted, the television coverage will have to be 'as directed'. In other words the direction of the shots will be ad libbed by the director as the programme develops.

Rehearsal

There might be some form of rehearsal for the show, but it would tend to be minimal as anything too well-rehearsed and detailed would destroy the freshness and spontaneity of the programme. The most that would happen in advance is the seating of the participants, the allocation of cameras and the working out in general of the size of shot each camera would undertake. Perhaps some of the questions or areas of discussion might be touched upon with the interviewee(s).

Counting down

The PAs first priority in the gallery would be to keep a keen eye on the time and count through the interview or discussion. She would know in advance how much time had been allocated to the item and she *must* keep everyone informed as to the length of time remaining.

Her counts would vary according to the length of the interview or discussion. If it is a short interview of only a minute or so duration she would have to give precise and frequent countdowns. But if the entire programme – say of 45.00″ duration – was a discussion then she should only give countdowns every 15.00″ until the final 15.00″. From then she should give warnings every 5.00″ and count down in the usual way from 1.00″ to the end of the programme.

As directed

Any 'as directed' sequence should be clearly stated as such when the PA is in the gallery and she should also name the cameras involved. From then on it might be helpful for her to inform the studio what is happening at each moment, e.g. 'on camera 3'.

Assisting director

In certain circumstances the PA could greatly assist the director by listening to the discussion and helping him assess what is likely to happen next. That sounds very much simpler than in fact it is because most PAs find that they emerge from a studio gallery with little or no knowledge of the content of the programme with which they have just been involved. This is especially true of the more technically complex programmes.

But in the studio discussion/interview situation this kind of assistance would be very helpful to the director.

'In certain circumstances the PA could greatly assist the director by listening to the discussion and helping him assess what is likely to happen next.'

Say, for example, the PA was involved in a programme comprising a panel of people answering questions from a studio audience. The audience would have been specially selected with groups representing specific interests. There would be a seating plan and the PA would know in advance where each group was seated and which camera was closest. By listening to the discussion and by constant reference to the seating plan she could advise the director, camera and boom operators should a shot be needed of a particular person or group.

Recorded programmes

If the programme is to be recorded with an editing session to follow, the PA should make notes for the editor, i.e. the questions asked, comments of particular interest, anything which definitely needs to be edited out of the final programme and so on.

Linking to next item

If the presenter is to close the interview/discussion with a scripted link from which the PA is to roll a pre-recorded item then she should be alert to any possible re-wording that the presenter might have to make in order to effect a smooth transition from the preceding item. If the link is unscripted then the onus is on the presenter to ad lib for the necessary time after the PA has rolled the item until it appears on the screen.

4

Outside broadcasts

We cannot leave the world of live television and move on to pre-recorded programmes without looking at live outside broadcasts and the role of the Production Assistant.

When television was still in its infancy, the outside broadcast represented one of the most exciting areas of the whole exciting new medium. The fact that the viewer could see the Cup Final of the football match, the grand State occasion, the gala variety show, as it was actually happening and usually from a better vantage point than the spectators at the event was, and still is, what television was all about for many people.

With the development of cable and satellite, the audience for these live events became world wide. On the 29th July 1981 when His Royal Highness Prince Charles married the Lady Diana Spencer in St Paul's Cathedral, London, live pictures were relayed to more than seventy countries, enabling over one eighth of the world's population to share in the occasion as it happened. On Saturday 13th July 1985 the Live Aid concerts at Wembley and Philadelphia in aid of famine relief involved eight satellites and reached an estimated audience of 1.5 billion – watching eighty-five percent of the world's television sets. For the Production Assistants sitting in the mobile control rooms at the heart of these massive spiders' webs of communication, these events must have posed awesome responsibilities.

But to separate outside broadcasts from other areas of television is, in some respects, misleading. The work of a PA on a live outside broadcast is very much defined by the nature of the programme. If the OB is of a variety show then her job would be very similar to that done by a PA working on the same type of show based in the studio. The same is true of many other outside broadcasts. Timing, rolling in pre-recorded items, counting in and out, logging, shot calling – all these elements might be and often are, involved. But there are instances where the work of the PA on a live outside broadcast differs from that of a PA working on a live studio-based programme and this is especially true in the areas which are very much the province of the live OB: sport and the large one-off event.

Involvement in programme content

Unlike the live news or magazine format programme where the PA's role is often restricted to one of time-keeping, on a live OB the PA is often closely involved not only in the research but also in the creative content of the programme.

Frequently there is only a producer (or director) and PA working on the programme and the PA is thus involved from the early setting up stages.

Preparing for the OB

The preparatory stage of a live OB involves the PA in a range of duties similar to the setting up of documentary filming. Dealing with people, making contacts, booking facilities, arranging transport and accommodation, liaison with the police, local authorities and countless other official bodies, getting archive material, attending planning meetings, compiling and typing out planning sheets, schedules, technical requirement details, the script and/or running orders are all standard tasks, many of which are gone into in detail in the next section of this book.

What is of paramount importance however is that the PA should familiarize herself as much as possible with what is to happen during the OB. This is because on many OBs there is one job of over-riding importance for the PA - a job known as 'living in the future'.

'The PA should familiarize herself as much as possible with what is to happen during the OB.'

Living in the future

In a live studio, the PA keeps everyone informed as to where they are in the running order of the programme. She counts through each item and warns the studio what is coming next.

On a scripted programme the PA will also talk the studio through the show largely by means of shot calling from the director's pre-planned camera script.

On a live outside broadcast which has no script and is largely dictated by the event itself, the PA's prime contribution is to provide a running commentary of the event, not by describing what is happening at that moment but by talking through what is to come.

The PA is able to provide this commentary by means of her detailed and intimate knowledge of the event. It means that she needs to have, not just a vague idea of the programme content but extremely well researched and memorized information.

For example, in an OB containing a ceremonial procession, the PA should know the route of the march, the order of the procession, the dignitaries involved. She should be able to put names to faces and recognize rank and title. She needs to be able to inform the director that 'X's car has just left the Town Hall' or that 'Y is just coming into shot on camera 5', with a certainty that it is X and Y and not A and B!

She needs, in fact, to learn the story of the event: the rules and regulations of each sport, the routine of the air display, the seating arrangements at St Paul's Cathedral etc. She needs to have attended rehearsals, on-site recces and planning meetings. The more information she has absorbed beforehand the more valuable will her contribution be during transmission.

Importance to directors

Many directors vision mix for themselves when working on a live OB. But whether they do their own vision mixing or not, their entire attention will naturally be taken up with what is immediate, what is happening at that moment. Their concentration is directed towards selecting the instantaneous shot and the one that is to come next. They rely on their PA for all the usual duties carried out by a PA in the gallery in addition to acting as a second pair of eyes by previewing the monitors which they are unable to concentrate on at that moment, especially when it is a large OB with many outputs.

Importance to camera operators

Isolated on scaffolding towers, positioned precariously on window-ledges or on rooftops, camera operators rely on the PA as their lifeline. They need to have warning of what is to come, of whether they are required to find a close up of a person or an exhibit and where that person or exhibit is to be found. They also need to know when the event has moved away from them giving them the opportunity to relax, especially in an event lasting some hours.

Importance to commentators

The man or woman in the commentary booth providing live commentary of the event is in a peculiarly vulnerable position. Many of them will welcome the advance information given by the PA.

Let us imagine that the commentator is about to talk about a rare floribunda at a flower show. The PA ought to be able to direct the camera operators to the correct plant. This would involve knowing what the plant looks like; knowing the layout of the show; it would mean having plans in front of her so that she knows which section of which stand in which part of the grounds the species is to be found. Then she will need to know which camera is closest to the plant.

But isn't that the director's job, you might well ask. Yes, but at that precise moment the director is engrossed in the immediate shots covering the judging of the roses. The commentator's talk will be the next item.

How to acquire that knowledge

How the PA obtains that intimate knowledge is very often a question of using her own ingenuity. There may be detailed rehearsals, but again there may not and the larger the event the less likelihood there would be for much rehearsing especially if the people involved are arriving from different parts of the world only the day or night before.

'How the PA obtains that intimate knowledge is very often a question of using her own ingenuity.'

Every OB is different and although the PA can build up a certain amount of experience over a period of time it must be remembered that the live OB is showing reality where anything and everything can happen. It is therefore essential that the PA is able to improvize, keep her wits about her and be able to cope under any circumstances.

Timing

Timing on a live OB can be critical, not so much in terms of getting the programme off the air, although that can be a priority, but often the timing within the OB itself can require a fine appreciation of the event and an ability to 'feel' the situation.

On sports events timing might or might not be important depending upon the sport and depending upon whether the OB is being transmitted as an entire programme or being inserted into a studio programme containing other live elements.

Timing within the sports event, however, might be essential. For example, how far into the match did the goal occur, or how long to go before the end of the boxing round? In wrestling matches the time-keeper might well be listening for the PA's count and she would therefore need an insert watch for each individual round and the interval as well as a master overall watch.

Physical stamina

Along with the ability to squeeze herself into a tiny space, cramped, confined and surrounded by people and equipment (if you are large or suffer from claustrophobia then steer clear of OBs!) the PA needs a certain amount of physical stamina especially when working on a live OB over several hours. She needs to be dextrous too in that there are far more telephones, keys and switches than in the studio gallery.

Communications

Communications form a vital part of the PA's job. She will be liaising constantly with everyone associated with the OB. She should never assume that information has been passed from one person to another but should always check for herself.

This again is standard PA work but whereas in the studio there is an advanced communications system with a full-time back-up staff of engineers, on OBs there will be a system – often ingenious in its complexity but sometimes tenuous in that it has to rely on cables stretching across muddy fields, telecommunications land lines that can be subject to interference or breakdown, cameras perched in remote spots and electricity supplies dependent upon the whims of generators. And instead of a back-up staff of unlimited numbers, all she will have is a small band of dedicated, harrassed engineers who have been up since the small hours trying to get it all to work!

Leaving nothing to chance

A PA's job on OBs therefore relies very much on all the standard skills of the PA plus a close involvement in the programme content plus an extra large dose of being able to adapt to anything at a moment's notice.

Because of the uncertain nature of most live OBs, few PAs working in them will leave anything to chance if they can check it beforehand. On a complicated variety show held one New Year's Eve, show business personalities, singers, dancers, politicians, anyone in the public eye and in London that night was to be brought into the studio or interviewed in the street during the course of the evening. It was to be one of those relaxed, unscripted programmes that look so simple when watching at home and are so complex if involved in the transmission.

For the PA, however, there was one detail that was of great importance and that was the necessity of cutting to a shot of Big Ben in time to see the great clock begin to chime prior to midnight. Because the cut to that shot was critical, on the night before transmission she was to be seen on Westminster Bridge at ten minutes to midnight, stopwatch in one hand, notebook in the other, ready to time Big Ben.

For any PA likely to need the same information, she found that at – 20″ to midnight there are run-up chimes which last for precisely 10″. At – 10″ there is silence lasting for 10″ and the first chimes are, as one would expect, on the stroke of midnight precisely.

'. . . ready to time Big Ben.'

5
Putting it all together

In the preceding chapters we have looked at the work of the PA in live programmes, isolating in turn the different elements that go to make up her job and paying especial attention to the demands made upon her in the gallery.

It is difficult, in a book, to fit it all together in terms of exactly how a PA conducts herself during a live transmission. Difficult because the experience needs to be gone through if not for real, then at least in a practical exercise.

But in order to give a flavour of what a PA does and says, step by step though a programme being transmitted live, we will work through the following imaginary programme of ten minutes duration. It is a simple show, with just four sequences:

		Estimated duration
1.	Opening titles (VTR)	30″
2.	Link into HIGHLAND GATHERING (VTR)	3.50″
3.	Link into studio INTERVIEW	4.30″
4.	Closing link into VISION OF THE HIGHLANDS (TC)	1.10″

For reasons of space I have typed the script in a continuous form; normally each sequence would be typed on a fresh page.

THE AFTERNOON PROGRAMME

/S/B VTR/

/ROLL VTR-2/ -5"

VTR- 2
OPENING TITLES

DURATION: 30"   S.O.VT

CAM 1   / Q MARY
MARY IN VISION   Good afternoon. In today's shortened
/S/B VTR-6/   version of The Afternoon Programme,

                                      we will be bringing you a report from

                                      the gathering of the McGuinness clan,

                                      followed by an exclusive interview with

                                      Hamish McGuinness, self-styled King of

                                      the Highlands. But to begin with,
            ROLL VTR-   John Tew reports from what must be one

                                      of the strangest gatherings in the
VTR-   western world./
HIGHLAND GATHERING

DURATION 3'50"
CAPGENS: Margaret McGuinness @ 1'05

          Colin McGuinness @ 2'25
                                      OUT WORDS: "..in all of Scotland"

/CAM 1 next/

```
CAM 1                              /Q  MARY
MARY IN VISION                     With us in the studio we have Hamish
                                   McGuinness, known to his clan as
CAM 2                              King of the Highlands./  Hamish,
2-s MARY AND HAMISH                where does the title come from?


CAMS 2 @ 3                         AS DIRECTED INTERVIEW

CAPGEN: Hamish McGuinness
DURATION:  4'30" approx.
/S/B TC/                                                    /S/B GRAMS/


CAM 1                          /  MARY
MARY IN VISION                    Well thank you very much indeed.  And
                                  that's all for today.  We'll be back
            ROLL TC               at the same time tomorrow with a rather
                                  different view of our national sport.
                                  Meanwhile we'll leave you with some
/S/B CLOSING CREDITS/             music and pictures of the misty
TELECINE                          Kingdom of the Highlands./  /GO GRAMS/
VISIONS OF THE HIGHLANDS
                                  CLOSING CREDITS
DURATION: 55"                     Presenter : Mary Calloway
                                  Director  : Len Greene
                                  Producer  : Philip Smith
```

```
DRAFT RUNNING ORDER    :    THE AFTERNOON PROGRAMME   :  WEDNESDAY 1 MAY 1985


In:    15.05.00                        Programme No: ABC/123/B
R/T:    10.00
Out:   15.15.00


Producer    :  Philip Smith         Presenter:  Mary Calloway
Director    :  Len Greene
P.A         :  Louise Blair
F.M         :  Fred Smith
```

SEQ.	SOURCE	TITLE	EST.	CUM.		
1	VTR	OPENING	0.30✓			
2	STUDIO (1) VTR + CAPS	Link into HIGHLAND GATHERING	3.50	4.20		
3	STUDIO (1) + (2) + CAP	Link into INTERVIEW WITH HAMISH McGUINNESS	4.30?	8.50		
4	STUDIO (1) TELECINE + CAPS	Closing link into⌐ 15" VISION OF THE HIGHLANDS ⌐ 55"	1.10 ✓			
				10.00		

Putting it all together. In a programme such as this, there is no point in backtiming. Sequence 4, comprising the closing link and film, has fixed times, which means that we must come out of the interview at 8.50.

Step by step guide

We shall start at one minute to transmission.

PA does	PA says	Script
		THE AFTERNOON PROGRAMME
Starts digital countdown clock having already liaised with presentation re. on air time and overall duration	'One minute to transmission, one minute'	
Possibly the director rehearses the opening of the insert items in which case she would count them down	45" to transmission, 45"	
	30" to transmission, 30" Standby VTR-2 with opening title	/S/B VTR/
	(VTR-2 beeps in response)	
Looks up to check ident on monitor displaying VTR-2	Thank you VTR	
Picks up overall stopwatch	15" to transmission, 15"	
Counts down from ident clock on monitor. Picks up insert watch	10"... 9 ... 8 ... 7 ... 6 ... ROLL VTR-2 ... 4 ... 3 ...	/ROLL VTR-2/ – 5 "
(Transmission screen goes blank)		
	2 ... 1 ... zero	VTR- 2
Starts both watches		OPENING TITLES

		DUR: 30"	S.O.VT
Puts master overall watch down Watches txn monitor and insert watch	On VTR for 30" Standby studio		
Counts off insert watch	15" left on VTR. Camera 1 next	/S/B CAM. 1/	
	10" on VTR		
	Counting out of VTR . . . 5 . . . 4 . . . 3 . . . 2 . . . 1 . . . zero		
Flicks insert watch back to zero and stops it while glancing at txn monitor to ensure VM has cut to studio. Notes down real time on r/o (Director cues Mary)		CAM 1 MARY IN VISION	MARY
	Stand by VTR-6 (VTR-6 beeps)		Good afternoon. In today's shortened version of the Afternoon
Looks up to check ident on monitor displaying VTR-6	Thank you VTR		programme, we will be bringing you a report from the gathering of the McGuinness clan, followed by an exclusive interview with Hamish McGuinness, self-styled King of the Highlands.

Script

MARY cont'd..
But, to begin with,
John Tew reports from
what must be one of the
strangest gatherings in
the western world./

ROLL-VTR-6

VTR
HIGHLAND GATHERING
DUR: 3'50'10
Capgens: Margaret McGuinness @ 1'05
         Colin McGuinness @ 2'25
out words: "in all of Scotland"

PA says

ROLL VTR-6
...4...3...2...1...zero

On VTR for 3'50" Standby first capgen 'Mary McGuinness'

Coming to capgen in
5...4...3...2...1...

(@ 1'10" into item)
3 minutes left on VTR, 3'

(@ 2'10" into item)
2 minutes left on VTR, 2' standby for capgen

PA does

Counts down from ident clock. Picks up insert watch

Starts insert watch as picture appears

(At that point the PA is handed a note saying that this insert runs for 4'10" She does not see any necessity to inform the studio because it would cause unneccessary confusion.)

She watches txn monitor as she is now not sure whether capgen timing is correct . . . it is!

She tells the producer that at the end of this item the programme will be overrunning by 40". The producer says to cut the interview down by 40"

She give a quick check that the name of the capgen is correct

PA tells director decision to cut interview by 40" then presses switch talkback key and tells presenter ...	Coming to capgen in 5 ... 4 ... 3 ... 2 ... 1 ...	CAM 1
		MARY IN VISION / MARY
	Mary, you've got just under four minutes for the interview	With us in the studio
(The presenter gives a thumbs-up sign to show she has understood.)		we have Hamish McGuinness,
	(@ 3'10" into item) 1 minute left on VTR, 1 minute. Out words are: 'in all of Scotland' Standby studio/standby camera 1	known to his clan as
	(@ 3'40" into item) 30" to studio, 30"	King of the Highlands../
	15" to studio, 15"	Hamish, where does the
	10" to studio, 10"	title come from?
Watches monitor as well as watch	Counting out of VTR ... 5 ... 4 ... 3 ... 2 ... 1 ... zero	
Notes down real time on r/o and works out final box	On camera 1, 2 next	CAM 2
On 2. As directed interview next		2-s

PA does	PA says	Script
(The director cues in the capgen of Hamish as soon as there is a single shot of him.)		AS DIRECTED INTERVIEW ON CAMS. 2 & 3
		Capgen: Hamish McGuinness
At this point the PA knows that she must come out of the interview at 8'50" in order to get off the air on time. Therefore she could use her insert watch for the interview, knowing that it must run no longer than 3'50", or she might opt to use her master overall watch to give the countdowns. She decides to use the master watch, therefore . . .		Duration: 4.30 approx. **3.50**
	(@ 5'50" into the programme) 3' left on the interview. 3'	
	(@ 6'50" into the programme) 2' left on the interview. 2'	
	(@ 7'50" into the programme) 1' left on the interview. 1'	
	Standby telecine/Standby grams	
	(Telecine responds)	
	Thank you	*S/B TC	S/B GRAMS*
She checks that the TC leader is set up	(@ 8'20" into the programme) 30" left on the interview. 30"	

Glances down at overall watch and notes time. They are running to time, thank goodness!

Counts down off telecine leader on monitor. Perhaps starts insert watch at zero but most probably would stay now with master watch

(The director cues in the closing credits)

(@ 8'35" into the programme)
15" left on interview.

10" wind up on interview

5 . . . 4 . . . 3 . . . 2 . . . 1

Telecine next

ROLL TELECINE . . .
. . . 7 . . .
. . . 6 . . .
. . . 5 . . .
. . . 4 . . .
. . . 3 . . .
. . . 2 . . . 1 . . . GO GRAMS

On telecine for 55"
Standby with closing credits

30" to end programme. 30"

15" to end. 15"

Counting out of programme
10 . . . 9 . . . 8 . . . 7 . . . 6 . . . 5 . . . 4
. . . 3 . . . 2 . . . 1 . . . zero. We're off air.

CAM 1
MARY IN VISION

Roll TC

TELECINE
VISIONS OF THE HIGHLANDS
DURATION 55"

CLOSING CREDITS

8'50 end interview

MARY
Well thank you very much indeed. And sadly, that's all for today. We'll be back at the same time tomorow with (a) rather different view of our national sport. Meanwhile we'll leave you with some music and pictures of the misty Kingdom of the Highlands./

9'05

CLOSING CREDITS

Presenter: Mary Calloway
Director: Len Greene
Producer: Philip Smith

10'00

Dos and donts in the studio gallery

This section is not solely for the PA working on live programmes. It is for all PAs involved in any studio gallery work. Whether the atmosphere in the studio is relaxed and good-humoured or whether it is nail-bitingly tense, there are certain ways of speaking and acting as a PA which should be adhered to. These are disciplines of speech and manner which should be learnt.

1. Do not speak unless you have something to say which is relevant to the programme. Some directors insist on a quiet, concentrated atmosphere while others favour a more casual approach. Whatever the individual director's style, you should remember that it is very confusing for everyone listening in to hear a lot of extraneous talk. In addition, the more your voice is heard talking about unimportant, unrelated matters, the less likely it is that people will take notice of you when you do say something pertinent and important.

2. When you need to speak, speak clearly and confidently. If you are too quiet you will not be heard and if you are too hesitant your instructions will lack conviction.

3. Always preface your remarks to the person intended to hear them. 'Fred on grams – would you pre-fade the music 5″ earlier', alerts Fred that you have something to say to him and he is then ready to take in your instruction. It also tells everyone else that the message is not for them. If you say, 'Pre-fade the music 5″ earlier would you Fred', Fred might not have realized that the message was intended for him until too late and everyone else would have had to listen to the whole message before realizing that it was not meant for them. After a bit they will cease to listen at all.

4. When giving a general warning you should repeat the vital part, if there is time, i.e. 'One minute to transmission, one minute'. It gives people who are busy with other things a second chance to hear your warning and fixes it firmly in their heads.

5. It is courteous to get to know the names of the camera operators and, indeed, everyone associated with the programme.

6. Try not to talk over the director. It can be difficult if a director is giving a long, complex note to, say the floor manager, and you have an urgent message, but it is rude to butt in; it will confuse those listening, especially the floor manager who will probably forget what the director has told him; it will infuriate the director and make for a very uncomfortable relationship. At least wait for the director to take a breath before you jump in.

7. You must always keep the studio informed about what is to happen next. It is not enough just to say: 'counting out of VTR . . . 5 . . . 4 . . . 3 . . . 2 . . . 1' without prefacing the count by saying: 'studio next', or 'coming to studio' or 'standby camera 3' or whatever. Each individual item leads on to something. At the end it leads to the end of the programme or coming off air and you should say so.

8. Whatever else you are engaged on, always keep an eye open for what the director is saying and for what is happening around you. Don't get so involved in your calculations that you are oblivious to everything else.

9. The situation can get pretty tense in the gallery and people can say things in the heat of the moment that they would afterwards regret. Be sure you never do so. Never, never swear. It can be understandable in certain conditions but is is not

clever, it will not gain you the respect of the studio and my advice is to leave it to others. Yours is the still, cool, calm voice in the midst of whatever furore is happening around you.

10. Try to keep a sense of proportion about the job. There is life outside the studio and if you can retain your sense of proportion and your sense of humour you will find it easier to cope. Don't forget that if you are finding yourself under a lot of pressure, so is the director.

11. Finally, if you are in the wrong, don't try to cover up or shelve responsibility on others. Too many people try to do that. Always admit your mistake and apologize.

'Always admit your mistakes . . .'

Hazards of the job

So just what can go wrong when working on live programmes? Well, almost anything and few galleries would run as simply and as smoothly as in the preceding chapter.

Problems, which ultimately end up in the gallery, can arise from many different sources:

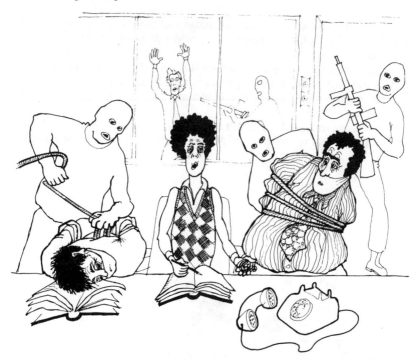

'Problems . . . can arise from many different sources . . .'

No time, no time!

For example:

☐ last minute script changes
☐ late arrival of edited inserts
☐ the running order being changed while on air
☐ the total abandonment of the running order because a major story has just broken.

More often than not this lack of time, this last minute rush, is because the programme needs to be as topical as possible and this is especially true of straight news programmes. If, as a PA, you cannot cope with this situation you should be working in another more leisurely area of television.

If, however, the live programme is not of this nature but there is nevertheless a terrible last minute panic it could indicate perhaps an indecisive producer, journalists and researchers who have got into lazy habits or a general unprofessionalism which might be worth examining in order to see whether the situation could be improved.

Technical problems

These can be caused by human error, e.g. the wrong insert item appearing on the screen, the wrong captions punched up or the right captions appearing over the wrong picture . . . the possibilities are endless. Sometimes these mistakes could be avoided by the PA making sure that she previews the monitors, checking for the shot that is to come next.

Technical problems can also be caused by circumstances beyond anyone's control. Machinery sticks, jams, breaks down. Considering the things that could go wrong it is, in one sense, amazing that so many live programmes occur without any apparent hitches.

Your priority, as PA, must be to get back on sequence whatever happens, and worry about the timings later.

Your own special problems

Apart from coping, within the limits of your responsibility, with any of the hazards cited above, you might well have a few personal ones of your own.

Forgetting to wind your watches

This should be one of your first tasks in the gallery, or before you go into the gallery.

Forgetting to start your master stopwatch

If this happens you can always work from the main studio clock, or from your digital countdown clock if you have one. You could also start your master watch at the end of the first sequence as you would have a definite timing for that.

Forgetting to start your insert watch

You can work out the timing from your master watch, i.e. at the end of the preceding sequence you have noted down the overall time to be 9.40″. The link into the insert is 10″, making the time you went into the insert 9.50″. The time now, on your master watch is 10.00″, therefore you must be 10″ into the insert.

You could start an insert watch at this point or work off the overall watch, i.e. if you went into the insert at 9.50″ and the duration of the insert is 1.10″ then your 'out' timing must be 11.00″. You can count out to that.

But supposing you did not note down the overall time at the end of the preceding sequence? Perhaps you were fully occupied with some last minute changes to the running order or some other crisis at the time. What you *do* know, however, is that the overall length of this particular insert is 2.40″. You would have a rough idea that you had let, say, 10″ to 15″ elapse before you (a) realized your error, (b) panicked, and (c) decided what to do. You could then give the studio an approximate idea of how long it was until the end of the item. 'We have roughly one minute left on VTR'. It is better than nothing. And do keep stressing the 'out' words.

An alternative might be to take your timing from the first capgen. Let us say that it is to be cued into the insert at 26″. You will, of course, be unable to cue it in but someone will do that, either the director, the producer or the reporter and you can then start your insert watch knowing that 26″ have elapsed since the start.

Forgetting to start your digital countdown clock

It is not a vital piece of equipment, provided you have other means of timing and use it as back-up only and an aid to getting off the air. If you forget to start it at the beginning of the programme, you could always start it late, providing you alter the countdown timing to coincide with the remaining length of the programme.

If your insert watch breaks down

You can work out where you are in the insert from your master watch using the method described above.

If your master stopwatch breaks down

You could work off the main clock. For example, if you know that the cumulative timing at the end of Sequence 11 was 8.35″ and your master watch has broken somewhere in the middle of Sequence 12, you know that your 'on air' time, was, say, 18.00.00 and that the time now, reading off the studio clock, is 18.09.35, you would therefore be 1.00″ into Sequence 12. You can then either work out the rest of your timings using real time or start another watch. Of course the examples I gave were simple and the timings would be far more complex than that, but if you grasp the system then you could put it into practice at need.

Alternatively you could work off your digital countdown clock, working out your backtimings from zero in order to match the time on the clock.

If the studio clock is inaccurate

You should always check, before the start of the programme, whether the studio clock is accurate. If it is a second or two fast or slow you could still work from it, adjusting your timings accordingly.

If the studio clock breaks down (and it has happened!)

If all your fail-safe systems fail, don't forget that you can always ring presentation. They will give you the duration to the end of the programme and you could start a watch from that, or they might give you a timing, say at ten minutes to the end, to enable you at least to bring the programme out smoothly.

If you have no accurate timing for the insert

If you know the timing is inaccurate you should give the studio the approximate timing and stress the 'out' words.

If you have no accurate timing for anything

You might go into the gallery with few, if any, timings. In that situation remember that the end of the programme is more important than the beginning. As soon as you can, start backtiming so that at least you come off air cleanly no matter what happens before.

If the running order is abandoned

It might well be changed on air for various reasons, in which case you adjust your timings and remember the advice above. If it is abandoned altogether it will be because of special circumstances, perhaps a major news story that has broken. Presentation might well allow you to be virtually open-ended with no fixed 'off air' time. If not, you should backtime from the known off air time and give the studio firm countdowns. If no-one heeds them, it is not your fault.

If your sums are wrong

Always double check your figures for it is vital that they are accurate. If you are wrong and realize your error in time, there is no harm done, although your confidence will be shaken. If your sums are wrong and you don't realize it until too late when you have perhaps crashed off the air, or been taken off by presentation, your options are:

- ☐ to go out and shoot yourself
- ☐ to hand in your resignation
- ☐ to determine to do better next time (if you are allowed a next time)!

Don't forget that everyone is human and subject to error and that even PAs are allowed to get things wrong once.

And after this horrendous programme where everything that could go wrong has gone wrong, I suggest you go home, have a good stiff drink, go to sleep and forget about it. Tomorrow's programme will go like a dream!

'. . . go to sleep and forget about it. Tomorrow's programme will go like a dream!'

Part Two

It'll be all right after it's edited: the flexible PA on recorded programmes

Multi- and single camera shooting

A theatre or concert-goer will see the entire performance from one angle only, from the seat he is occupying in relation to the stage. He may have a good, clear, unobstructed view of the stage or his enjoyment may be marred by having to crick his neck at an awkward angle because some object is obscuring his vision. At all events, unless he gets up and moves from his seat to an unoccupied one elsewhere, he will have only one view of the stage and a wide angle one at that.

But while that is perfectly acceptable in the theatre and at concerts it would prove very boring if television were shown from one angle only.

This discovery is not, of course, new to television. Years before, the development of film gave rise to a new art form, whereby through the juxtaposition of shots of different sizes and angle, creatively edited together to form a smooth-flowing composite whole, the audience is guided through the story, seeing it, in a sense, through the eyes of the director's interpretation of the script. In order to achieve that effect the technique of single camera, out of sequence shooting was employed.

Single camera shooting

Shooting out of sequence using only one camera means that the script is not generally shot in strict chronological order. Scenes are shot according to factors such as the availability of actors, different locations, ease of setting up etc., all determined by over-riding considerations such as the budget and speed of shooting.

But not only are scenes shot out of order. Because only one camera is involved, shots within each scene are also taken out of order, the entire scene, or parts of it, being repeated for the camera to record different angles and shot sizes.

This entire mass of disjointed shots, rather resembling the pieces of a jigsaw puzzle when the box is opened, are then assembled by an editor in the correct story order with the individual shots creatively spliced together in order to give dramatic meaning and pace to the film.

This method of shooting allows a great deal of flexibility at all stages of the production. Although any good director will plan his shots with an ultimate concept of the finished work in mind, there is room for experimenting, for change both during filming and, most importantly, in the editing stage.

Multi-camera shooting

Because television was originally either live or pre-recorded on film, the live element was, by its very nature, unable to adopt the film technique of out of sequence shooting because there was no possibility of post production work before the programme was transmitted.

So there remained the alternative of transmitting a programme which used a single camera rather in the manner of a member of the audience at the theatre seeing the programme from one angle and one shot size only, or evolving a system whereby the viewer would see the programme through a series of differing shots and angles, as they would a film, but which could be transmitted live.

The answer was, of course, to use a number of cameras simultaneously. Each camera would be positioned in the studio to give shots from pre-arranged angles. The work of each camera would be plotted beforehand by the director on to a camera script and in the control room of the studio the vision mixer would cut instantaneously from one camera to another in order, according to a pre-determined script. This would straightway give a succession of shots of different size and angle while showing the scene played through in story order.

Advantages and disadvantages

The technique of multi-camera shooting has its advantages and disadvantages like everything else. One advantage is that actors and performers are able to give more consistent performances than with single camera shooting. In addition, the days spent in the studio produce a finished entity.

Its main disadvantage, however, lies in the rigidity of the system in which everything has to be pre-planned to a degree that some directors find unacceptable as it allows very little flexibility when recording the programme.

When videotape came into common use in television it was possible for post-production editing to take place. But because, in its infancy, videotape editing was cumbersome if not primitive, the multi-camera system was widely used for all manner of television programmes with only the minimum of editing afterwards.

Multi-camera shooting.

Nowadays, with the greater sophistication of editing on tape, it is becoming more and more possible to combine some of the freedom of the film-style technique while recording on to videotape.

The need for flexibility

This means that the PA needs to have a greater flexibility of approach than hitherto. It is very possible for studio or outside broadcast productions to be recorded in whole or in part with one camera only and for the sections shot multi-camera to be recorded out of sequence. This necessitates a degree of continuity to be observed on the part of the PA together with accurate recording notes compiled for the editing.

These aspects will be examined more fully later on in this section of the book. First, we will look at the PAs job on multi-camera productions, taking a fictitious drama as our base.

As it is always sensible, wherever possible, to start at the beginning, I would like you to imagine an office, equipped with the sort of furniture found in any office – desks, telephones, typewriter, shelves, filing cabinets . . .

6

In the beginning ...

You have been assigned to work with X - a director of many years experience in the industry - on a six part drama series. You arrive before X - the PA is frequently the first person on a production in its intensive setting up period, although a certain amount of preparatory work will already have been done: a budget allocated; the scripts commissioned and a format decided upon. In this case it is to be primarily studio based with the exteriors shot as an outside broadcast.

So you know something about the production you are about to work on. What – after re-arranging the desks and furniture more to your liking - do you do next?

One of your main jobs in this setting up period will be to act as central co-ordinator for the programme. In the weeks to come you will amass quite an amazing amount of paperwork, some of it generated by yourself as you book various facilities, some of it by others associated with the production.

If an army is reputed to march on its stomach then the average television production marches along a road paved with memos, requisitions and paperwork in general. This is not true of all companies or all programmes but there is usually a vast number of forms, the greater part generated by the PA.

Word processors are being used by some companies, their aim being to save much of the repetitious drudge of typing and re-typing as well as trying to abolish much of the paper that clogs up the internal post, the desks and the filing cabinets of the building.

It is not possible to go into the exact number and type of form that will require filling in. Every company has its own system and a new PA should follow precedents set by previous ones. Some companies have their own pre-printed forms whereas other leave the setting out to the discretion of their PAs.

What I have done is to take a representative sample of forms and list them under the headings of future chapters in order to give some idea of exactly what is involved in this purely administrative side of the job.

Initial paperwork

The programme file

As it is essential that all this paperwork be kept and filed in an easily retrievable fashion one of your first jobs should be to open a programme file - the Bible of the production.

'. . . the average television production marches along a road paved with memos, requisitions and paperwork in general.'

Apart from the programme file, there are other jobs which will claim your early attention. In no special order they are:

Production number

The programme will be assigned a production (or job) number. You should find out what it is and use it as a reference on any paperwork.

Stationery

You should ensure that you have an adequate supply of stationery for the weeks ahead.

List of personnel

You should find out the names of as many people as possible who will be working on the production. Type out a list, together with their addresses and telephone numbers and circulate to all concerned.

Distribution list

Your company will most probably have a distribution list, i.e. a list of the people to whom you need to send scripts, memos, booking forms and so on. As these vary from company to company it is not possible to give any standard for reference.

Check list

You should obtain a copy of the departmental check list for PAs. If no such list exists you might find it helpful to compile one for yourself as it is a very useful aide memoire.

All this is, of course just good secretarial work but one of your functions as PA is to be a good secretary and it is not an aspect of the job to be despised.

Once you have informed the telephone operator of your existence and typed and pinned up a label for the production office door you sit back and await the arrival of your director and production team.

'. . . you sit back and await the arrival of your director and production team.'

The production team

A whole army of people are employed at different stages during the making of a television programme and any production is the result of the coming together of a whole range of creative talent.

The core of this army is the production team, comprising those people who will work almost, if not totally, exclusively on this particular programme. Their number can vary depending upon the requirements of the programme and the way the jobs are defined within the company. Their titles, too, vary from company to company and this can cause confusion. However the key personnel would contain the following:

The producer

For our six-part series there may well be an executive producer as well as producer who would carry overall responsibility for the production under the departmental head. If there is no executive producer, the producer carries out this function. He/she frequently commissions the scripts, might be responsible for engaging the director and is closely involved in casting. He/she has overall responsibility for bringing the programme in within the budget allotted and time span agreed. The producer might or might not have to work out the initial budget and allocation of facilities or that might be the job of the production associate.

Production associate

The production associate is responsible for the overall budget and for booking basic facilities, i.e. studios, OB crews, etc. They also have the thankless task of trying to keep the rest of the production team within the confines of both budget and time scale allocated.

The writer

The writer is not technically part of the production team but it would seem churlish to leave him or her off our list of key personnel! The writer's work will, hopefully, be finished by the time the production team swing into action, but all too often the writing and re-writing is still taking place well into the setting up period to the frustration of everyone and the added workload of the PA. It is not all the writer's fault, however, for ensuring that the rehearsal scripts are finished in good time is largely the responsibility of the story editor.

Story editor (also known as script editor)

Sometimes the producer takes on this function but frequently there is a separate story editor whose job it is to guide the writer through the hazards and pitfalls of writing for television. They need to provide both support and criticism where necessary based on their expert knowledge of the television medium and ensure that the writing is to the specified time slot.

The director

The director's responsibility is to the script. He (and I must stress that I use the pronoun to cover both sexes) provides the creative interpretation of the script, turning the printed page into the pictures and words that form a television production. The director must be a creative person, sensitive to the writer's intentions whilst exercising his own craft. He must have a good understanding of the mechanics of television production. He must be able to inspire actors as well as the production team with his image of the finished work: he must be able to communicate ideas and be receptive to the ideas of others. The director must be able to weld together the disparate talents of his team to form a harmonious whole. The director should inspire confidence as well as exhibiting all the qualities of leadership including the single-minded ruthlessness to get the job done.

And if the above paragraph does not equate with any directors that you know personally, remember that we all fall very far short of the ideal!

Directors vary in sex, in shape, in age, in temperament, in experience. There is no typical director just as there is no typical PA or anyone else.

Because the PA works very closely to and with the director – in some respects the job could well be termed 'Director's Assistant' rather than 'Production Assistant' – this liaison can be fruitful and very much to the benefit of the production as a whole, or it can be uneasy if not damaging.

Designer

The designer is responsible for the overall design of the set, whether studio or on location and will work in conjunction with the director to create the mood and atmosphere of the production.

Floor manager

The floor manager joins the production some time before rehearsals begin and is, in effect, the first assistant director. He or she will work closely with the director and actors, directing extras, issuing artists' call times and working out the recording order on studio days. The floor manager will be in overall charge of the studio floor. Sometimes the FM will work out the schedule for outside broadcast recording, sometimes the production assistant will do this job, but they will work in close liaison. The floor manager will normally go filming or out on OBs.

Location manager

The location manager finds venues for location work, whether film or OB, negotiates payments for the use of locations and is generally in charge of this aspect during the shooting.

Some companies combine the jobs of floor manager and location manager in the person of the production manager.

Production manager

The production manager carries out the work of the floor manager and location manager. He/she is closely involved with the programme, often starting work on it at about the same time as the PA.

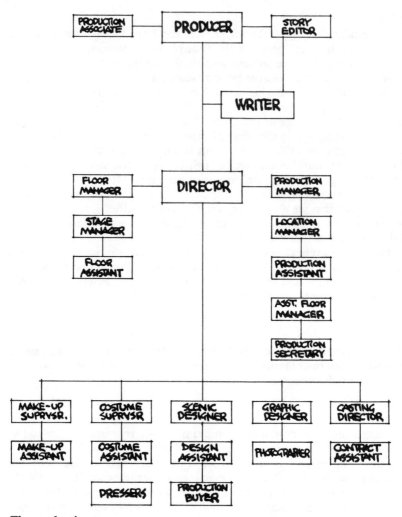

The production team.

Stage manager (also known as assistant floor manager)

The stage manager is responsible for any action props, for prompting artists, for cueing when required, for updating the script and for continuity in the studio. Their role is that of second assistant director.

Floor assistant

Is the call boy and works directly to the floor manager in calling the artists when needed and carrying out any other function assigned by the FM.

Casting director

The casting director has a specialized knowledge of actors and will work closely with the director in casting the production. The casting director will suggest possible actors for the different parts, will find out their availability, will arrange auditions and will book the actors. If there is no casting director this job is done by the director, assisted on occasion by the production manager together with the PA.

Costume supervisor

Is responsible for the design of the artists' costumes. The costume supervisor will have an assistant during the setting up period and dressers will be assigned to the show on production days.

Make-up supervisor

Is responsible for the artists' make-up and will have one or more assistants during production days.

Graphic designer

Will be responsible for opening and closing titles and any other art work for the production.

Production buyer (also known as properties buyer)

Is responsible for the hire or purchase of set dressing and will work closely with the set designer.

Production secretary (also known as producer's secretary)

A production secretary's work will often overlap with that of the PA. Frequently they will work to the producer, typing the rehearsal scripts, budgets, etc., and have much to do with the early preliminary work of setting up the production.

All these people will be involved to a greater or lesser extent with the setting up of your production. There are also the studio and OB personnel, some of whom will only be involved during the actual production days but their chiefs will attend planning meetings and technical run-throughs.

Wall charts, rehearsal scripts and schedules

'Which came first, the chicken or the egg?' is an old saying and one which could be accurately applied to almost any production in the setting up period.

Some people would assert that no constructive work could be done before the scripts have been finalized. But anyone who has worked in production will know that work often starts on a programme without the final scripts – sometimes without any scripts at all, purely an outline of the story and a list of characters.

It can be difficult to assess the number of days rehearsal, OB, film and studio required until the scripts are in a finished form and therefore difficult to schedule the weeks ahead, but it may well be that the studio has had to be booked months in advance, ditto the OB crews. It will then be more a question of fitting the scripts into the pre-allocated facilities rather than tailoring the facilities to fit the scripts.

Whatever the situation pertaining to your production, you should, as in all PA work, do what you can when you can, and one thing you can do fairly early on is provide wall charts.

Wall charts

1. Day by day

First of all a chart showing each day of the production should be made. This chart can be manufactured using different coloured cards – each card representing one day and the different colours clearly showing rehearsal days, studio days, OBs and so on. If your company has specially designed charts you should of course use them.

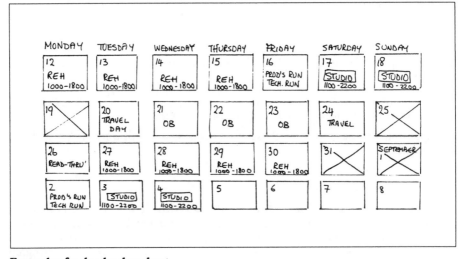

Example of a day by day chart.

Any information relevant to the production should be written on the chart and kept up to date daily. Meetings, recces, travel days, days off – everything should be shown.

2. Production list

The names, addresses and telephone numbers of the production team should be written in large letters on another chart.

3. Artists' chart

The movement of artists – whether travelling, rehearsing, on location, in the studio, costume fitting, make-up, photo-calls, etc. can with a large cast, become

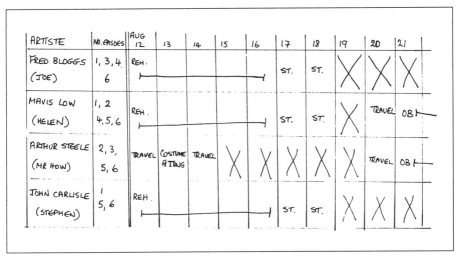

ARTISTE	NO. EPISODES	AUG 12	13	14	15	16	17	18	19	20	21
FRED BLOGGS (JOE)	1, 3, 4 6	REH.					ST.	ST.	X	X	X
MAVIS LOW (HELEN)	1, 2 4, 5, 6	REH.					ST.	ST.	X	TRAVEL	OB
ARTHUR STEELE (MR HOW)	2, 3 5, 6	TRAVEL	COSTUME FITTING	TRAVEL	X	X	X	X	X	TRAVEL	OB
JOHN CARLISLE (STEPHEN)	1 5, 6	REH.					ST.	ST.	X	X	X

Example of an artists' chart.

extremely complicated. The only way to keep track of them is by another chart which will show you at a glance who is doing what, where, on each day and will prove invaluable in working out supplementary payments.

Rehearsal scripts

However the original manuscript is delivered – handwritten on the backs of old cigarette packets or typed out with painstaking care – it will be necessary for either the PA or the production secretary to re-type it in an acceptable form as a television rehearsal script.

Format
(a) Scripts should be typed on one side of the page only.
(b) The typing should be on the righthand side of the page to enable the director to plot in his cameras on the left. It is not helpful to type stage directions on the lefthand side.
(c) Plenty of space should be given between the lines of dialogue and stage directions should be easily distinguishable from the dialogue by typing them in capitals.
(d) Page numbering should be consecutive.
(e) Each scene should be started on a fresh page. This will make it easier for re-writes and amendments to be slipped into the body of the script and is *essential* for working out schedules.
(f) If you are working on a series, then in addition to the consecutive page numbering the PA should identify each page with its episode and scene number, i.e. Ep.2/Sc.3, or, more simply, II/3.

Scenes

In an earlier part of the book I wrote that everything in television is broken down into manageable sections. Scripts should be likewise broken down into scenes, if the writer has not already done so, each scene being a different set or location. The scenes should be numbered and the heading state whether an interior or exterior and the time of day.

i.e.   SCENE 1: DAY. INT. CELLAR

SCENE 2: DAY. INT. HALL

Example of rehearsal script

– 10 –   IV/4

SCENE 4: NIGHT. EXT. GARDEN (BY SUMMER-HOUSE)

THE SUMMERHOUSE IS ABLAZE WITH LIGHT, SENDING LONG SHADOWS ACROSS THE LAWN, TREES AND SHRUBS. SILHOUETTED AGAINST THE HOUSE IS LOUIS, WHO WATCHES ALICE MAKE HER WAY TO MEET HIM.

ALICE
I'm sorry . . . I couldn't come sooner . . .

LOUIS
I hardly expected you at all – after what's happened . . .

ALICE
So you know?

LOUIS
Yes. Here . . . sit down . . .

HE HELPS HER TO A SEAT

Colour coding

If you are working on a series then it is extremely helpful to employ a colour coding system. Each rehearsal script should be duplicated on different coloured paper, the same colours carried through the script breakdowns, schedules and so on.

Distribution

Whether or not you typed the rehearsal script, it is the PA's job to ensure that it is sent to all the relevant people – not forgetting the writer!

Your next job will then be to break the script down into a simple chart known as the breakdown.

Script breakdown

An example of a script breakdown is given below. Note that a synopsis of the scene is given. This will prove invaluable, especially when you are working on more than one script.

Page No.	Scene No.	Int/Ext	Day/Night	Location	Characters	Synopsis	Sp. requirements
1	1	Int	Day	Railway Stn.	Louis Alice Porter (W.On) Passengers	She meets him off train Arrange meeting in garden	F/P train
3	2	Ext	Day	Gravel pit	Ch.Insp. Bartley James Wilcox Policemen	Police find body	Body of Ashley Tew
4	3	Int	Night	Dining Room at Manners House	Alice John James Wilcox Mary Wilcox Elwyn Brand Grant Tyler Sarah Glyn	Dinner party where Alice finds out about Tew - is regarded with suspicion by James. Sarah and John exchange speaking glances!	
10	4	Ext	Night	Garden (by summerhouse)	Alice Louis	They meet. She tells him of her fears. He dismisses them.	

Example of a script breakdown.

Schedules

Schedules are the creative effort of the immediate production team and are issued for everything: rehearsals, filming, OBs, studios. Sometimes they are worked out solely by the PA, sometimes by the floor manager (or production manager). The director, too, has a say in the schedule but the end product is the result of expertise in compilation and organization of the salient facts, placing them in a simple to understand and comprehensive order, and that is the responsibility of the PA. On a complex programme the schedules can be works of art!

Rehearsal schedules

Normally the director and/or floor manager will work out the schedule, based on the amount of rehearsal the director wishes to allocate to each scene.

This schedule is usually simple and straightforward with dates, times, venues and artistes involved, together with perhaps any special props needed as a reminder to the stage manager.

OB schedules

Depending on the length and complexity of the OB, this schedule could comprise many pages.

1. The cover page will contain the series title, the production number(s), the names, room and telephone numbers of the production team and details of the crew. It will also contain the distribution list, unless this is shown on a separate sheet.

Then, in no special order, there will be the following information:

2. Details of locations, dates, times, addresses, contacts and parking.
3. The actors involved in the OB, the dates required and episodes each one will appear in.
4. Technical information specific to the OB.
5. Accommodation details for cast and production.
6. Travel details for cast and production.
7. Catering information.
8. Useful contacts.

There will then be a comprehensive day-to-a-page breakdown of the OB giving each day:

(a) the location
(b) the call times
(c) the names, addresses and telephone numbers of the contacts for that day
(d) catering arrangements
(e) transport arrangements
(f) directions to locations
(g) an hour by hour schedule of recording
(h) the order of recording with scene breakdowns.

At the back will be attached relevant maps with the locations circled.

MONDAY 2 SEPTEMBER

LOCATION:	THE OLD MILL HOUSE, Grangeley, Kent
CONTACT:	Mr G. LEADER (Caretaker) Tel: Grangeley 465
LOCATION CATERERS:	Fosley & Cole (Tel: 789 1234)
UNIT TRANSPORT:	As Location Manager's sheet
DIRECTIONS:	On entering Grangeley from the north, take the 2nd left at the roundabout into Lowescroft Road. Follow road to T-junction. Turn right into Shadley Road. 3rd left into Grangeley Avenue and the Old Mill House is immediately on your right.
CALL TIMES:	0800 at Lowescroft Hotel (for costume and make-up):

HELEN DEWSBURY (Joan)
CHRISTINE SHALTON (Harriet)
SUSANNA SHAW (Sarah)
ROGER SHINER (Harry)
PETER JOHNS (Graveney)

0915 R.V. ON LOCATION : Crew and artistes

1400   JOANNA STUART (Vicky) - driver to collect from
         hotel)

SCHEDULE: 0930-1300 SHOOT I/6, I/9
             1300-1400 LUNCH
             1400-1715 SHOOT III/1, IV/7
             1715   WRAP

SHOOTING ORDER:

Ep/Scene	Pages	Int/Ext Time	Location	Characters	Cameras	Shots
I/6	1-4	Ext/Day	Garden by stream	Joan Harry Graveney	1, 2, 3	1-12
I/9	5	"	"	Harriet/Sarah	1, 2	13-18
III/1	6-9	"	Garden by mill wheel	Harry/Graveney Joan	1, 2, 3	19-29
IV/7	10-11	"	"	Vicky/Harriet	1, 2	30-36

Example of an OB schedule (day to a page). NB The script page numbers will have been over-written to be consecutive for the OB shooting for the sake of simplicity on the OB.

Order of recording

The order of recording will normally be worked out with reference to a number of criteria:

☐ the number of scenes at any one location
☐ the position of locations, bearing in mind travel needs
☐ the availability of locations
☐ the availability of actors
☐ the number of days allocated to the OB

Studio schedules

These form part of the camera script as the recording or running order and will be explained in detail in Chapter 7.

The planning meeting and further programme requirements

Representative sample of forms

Technical requirements
Visual effects
Scenic projection
Studio information:
  fire hazards
  gas/water
  wind/rain
  chemicals
  electrics
  animals
Costume and make-up details
Properties and drapes
VTR and telecine booking requirements
Studio day facilities:
  studio audience
  restaurant facilities
  request for teleprompt and/or caption generator
Graphic design requisition
Musical requirements
Sound recording sheet
Recorded music – tape usage
Music and effects dubbing requirements
Music cue sheet
Petty cash
Expenses claim
Producers' final estimate

If you find the above list daunting, I am afraid it by no means covers all the things you might be required to book/arrange/organize as a PA. It will do, however, to give you an idea of the range of administrative duties.

Planning meeting

Once a date has been set for the planning meeting, the PA will notify all members of the production team together with the senior technical studio staff.

The designer would normally bring scale models of the studio sets to the meeting together with the floor plan to enable everyone to see exactly what will be involved.

The director will then talk through the production and discuss all aspects: the technical requirements, cameras, sound, special effects; costume and make-up requirements; design; the recording schedule and so on. Any problems will be discussed and fully thrashed out.

During this meeting the PA will take notes and circulate the decisions reached to everyone who attended.

OB planning meeting

A similar meeting will be held for the OB engineering staff and production team either in the production office or 'on site', i.e. at the location where the OB is to be held. At this meeting the location manager will outline the schedule and all the technical requirements for the OB will be itemized.

'The director will talk through the production . . .'

Costume and make-up

Both the costume and make-up supervisors will want breakdowns from the director of the production requirements. They will also require a full cast list with addresses and telephone numbers of the artists.

Properties and drapes

It is usually *not* the responsibility of the PA to fill in the forms relating to properties and drapes.

VTR and telecine bookings

The PA will probably have to book the required VTR facilities, both for the recording itself and the post production work of editing and dubbing. If VHS copies are required for viewing or off-line editing purposes, the PA must book those as well, requesting burnt-in time code.

If film inserts are to be played into the studio the PA will have to book telecine, giving dates and times needed.

Studio day facilities

The PA will need to make catering arrangements for the studio crew and cast by informing the canteen or restaurant of the numbers involved and the dates and times of the meal breaks.

Studio audience

If there is to be an audience in the studio, the PA will need to inform reception, the commissionaires, the security staff and the studio operatives. The PA might have been involved in getting together the audience: by advertisements in the press, by contacting interested organizations or by other means. Alternatively this job might be done by another person who will then need to know the type and size of audience required.

Graphic design

The PA will fill in the required graphics forms, providing details of the front titles and end credits. The information will be provided after discussions between the graphic designer and director. It is naturally very important for the PA to check the spelling of the actors and production members entitled to a credit as she will not be at all popular if names are mis-spelt on air. She should also check abbreviations: someone known as Chris might well wish his name to be Christopher on the credits.

Music requirements

The PA needs to tread very cautiously when it comes to booking musicians. It would not be appreciated if she fills the studio with a symphony orchestra when all the director wanted was a small string ensemble!

Music played live in the studio *must* be cleared for copyright purposes *before* the studio and any recorded music, e.g. gramophone records, must likewise be cleared. The type of clearance required should be checked first, i.e. for transmission in one country or world clearance. You will also need to know whether the music is 'visual', i.e. the actors can 'hear' it, or 'background', i.e. mood music to create an atmosphere which the actors on the production cannot 'hear'.

The copyright laws are designed to give protection to the person or organization who has created the work and these laws are rightly strict.

Finance

The PA would not normally be responsible for the production budget, but might be held responsible for the day to day running costs and might be required to fill in a form at the end of the production showing these costs.

'The PA might have been involved in getting together the audience.'

Actors and rehearsals

Representative sample of forms

Artists' booking form
Extras' booking form
Rehearsal time sheet
Dressing room allocation form

Artists' studio call sheet
Artists' time sheet
Children's time sheet
Extension of role (extras and walk-ons)
Supplementary payments receipt form
Release of artists' fees
Rehearsal room booking form
Outside rehearsal requirements
Props required for rehearsal

Booking artists

If there is a casting director, the PA will have little to do with the selection of actors, with auditions and so on. If there is no casting director the PA will probably be required to assist the director in checking artists' availability, in arranging auditions – making sure that scripts are available – and sometimes in attending the auditions.

Once the director has selected his cast, the PA will ensure that they are contracted by sending a form to the relevant department. This form should contain as much information as possible:

☐ the character which the actor is required to play;
☐ the overall length of the engagement;
☐ the number of episodes in which the actor will appear (if a series);
☐ the studio/filming/OB dates;
☐ rehearsal dates;
☐ in the case of a series, whether the recordings will be one episode at a time or multi-episodic, i.e. on one studio day scenes from a number of different episodes to be recorded.

She should also note whether the contract is to contain any special clauses, i.e. that hair should/should not be cut, that a beard or moustache should be grown.

If the programme is to be a co-production, that also should be noted on the form.

Once the contract has been issued a copy will be sent to the PA who should read it through to ensure that it is accurate on all points.

Booking stuntmen

In addition to the above information, the PA should write down the nature of the stunt that is to be performed.

Booking extras/walk-ons

Extras and walk-ons are non-speaking parts or characters who may or may not, have a few unscripted words or lines to say.

Working from the director's requirements, the PA will fill in a form for extras and walk-ons, stating the number required, dates, times and places, whether male or female, the approximate ages and type, i.e. farm labourers, assorted office workers and so on.

Employment of children

There are strict laws in the UK governing the employment of children, i.e. those under the age of 16. These should be read and understood by any production assistant who needs children in their cast and the schedules worked out accordingly. It will be necessary to engage chaperones and tutors and the children's hours of work and study will be strictly regulated. It is generally the PA's job to keep a note of the hours for submission to the inspector.

Cast list

Once the cast has been finalized and booked, the PA should type out two lists, one a simple cast list for general distribution, the other a more detailed list with addresses, telephone numbers, agents' names and telephone numbers, the episodes in which the actors will appear and the dates for which they have been contracted. Distribution of this list should be restricted to the relevant members of the production team, i.e. the producer, floor manager, costume and make-up supervisors.

Information to cast

The PA will then write to the actors with the following details:

(a) scripts
(b) time and place of the read-through
(c) times and places of:
        rehearsals,
        location filming/OB (sending a schedule if it exists at that stage),
        studio dates
(d) maps as necessary to get to the rehearsal room/location/studio
(e) details of accommodation if it has been necessary to book it.

Time sheets/studio call sheets

Either you or the floor manager will keep a note of the hours and days worked by the artists and extras. You will probably have to type out this list either at weekly intervals or at the end of the production and send it to the relevant department for supplementary payments for additional hours and days worked.

Photo calls

The PA might be required to book photocalls - arranging the photographer and the venue and ensuring that the actors are informed and any arrangements made for travel where necessary.

Dressing rooms

Once the studio schedule is worked out it will be necessary for the PA to book dressing rooms for the cast.

'The first time the entire cast is assembled together will be for the read-through.'

Read-through

The first time the entire cast is assembled together will be for the read-through. It is the PA's responsibility to book the room in which the read-through is to take place; to ensure that everyone has been notified of time and place and that scripts have been sent to the cast well in advance.

Read-through timings

The timings on a recorded programme are naturally more fluid than on a programme going out live, but they are important, nonetheless. During the read-through the PA should note down the timings in pencil on each page of script. She should also write down the running time of each scene and add them together cumulatively to give a rough overall running time. It should be stressed that this will only be an approximate timing, but if the slot allotted for the programme is fifty minutes and the read-through lasts three hours, she would be wise to inform the director!

In any case she will probably have a good idea already about the overall length of the scripts. If the rehearsal scripts are typed using the layout suggested earlier then fifty such pages containing a mixture of action and dialogue will work out at roughly half an hour of screen time.

Rehearsals

It would be unlikely for the PA to attend many of the rehearsals unless specifically requested by the director.

The stage manager and floor manager attend rehearsals and any script changes will be noted by the stage manager who will pass them on for re-writes and incorporation into the final camera script. The SM will also keep a note of the artists' hours and time the scenes more accurately.

Blocking

During the rehearsals the director will 'block' the scenes, working out both actors' moves and positions and the moves and positions of his cameras.

Floor plan

The camera positions will be plotted by the director on a studio floor plan, the sets having been drawn by the designer after discussions with the director. Copies of this floor plan will then be distributed to the studio staff.

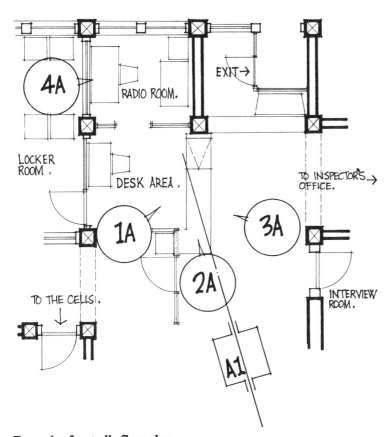

Example of a studio floor plan.

Camera notes on script

During the course of the rehearsals the director will be marking the cutting points from one camera to another on his script and noting down the kind of shots he wants from each camera position. This will eventually form the basis of the camera script which is described in the next chapter.

Producer's run and technical run

The culmination of the rehearsal period is the producer's run and technical run when the scenes are acted in the order they will be recorded in the studio for the benefit of the production team and technical studio staff.

The director will point out camera positions and moves, lighting and sound and any problems will, hopefully, be resolved before the production goes into the studio.

7

The camera script

In a multi-camera production, the director needs to have worked out the visual and sound coverage well in advance of the studio day. He needs to have assessed the number of cameras required, where they will be positioned initially, where they will move to during the course of the action – taking care that he does not get their cables hopelessly entangled in the process. He needs to have worked out the precise cutting points from one camera to another and to have thought out in advance the type of shots he wants.

All this is worked out during the rehearsals. With the aid of the studio floor plan and models of the sets the director will establish the moves and positions of the actors and the shots will become fixed in his mind. Most directors note this information down on their rehearsal scripts and this will eventually be passed to the PA to type out in the form of a camera script.

The camera script is therefore a very important document, representing a total handbook of the director's concept of the programme. Certain details might of course change both before and during the studio – shots will alter, cameras change, actors be re-positioned – that is all part of the creative process. But any director going into a multi-camera studio situation without a prepared camera script is asking for trouble, unless of course he has planned for an 'as directed' sequence for a specific reason – perhaps because the shots cannot be anticipated in advance.

So at some stage in the setting up of a production, usually at the latest possible moment, the PA will be handed a document which might well be dog-eared and tatty with more or less legible handwriting scrawled over it, see the example on page 112. And a word of warning here. It is vital that the PA set a deadline to the director for the script. Not something unrealistic from the director's point of view, but an agreed date allowing the director sufficient time to prepare the script and the PA time to type it and get copies duplicated.

Front pages

Although the body of the camera script will be made up of the director's instructions typed on to the rehearsal script, the front pages will consist of information worked out by the PA either by herself or in conjunction with the floor manager.

111

51 **1B**
WS Sue L frame
Lesley R

Grab L. Hold
or tite to
MS Lesley

52 **2A**
MS Sue

53 **1B**
MS L.

54 **2A**
MSS

54 **1B**
MS L
Hold her as she sits

Tite to MCU

55 **2A**
MWS

SCENE 10

INT. DAY. OFFICE

SUE IS SITTING AT AN OFFICE DESK.
LESLEY IS PACING UP AND DOWN.

LESLEY

Well I said to him - you can't have
it both ways Trevor - you've got to
get your priorities straight my lad
- either we have a serious, meaningful
relationship, or I don't want to know.

SUE

What did he say?

LESLEY

He said he didn't want to get involved.
I mean, honestly!

SUE

So what did you say?

LESLEY (SITTING DOWN)

Well I said - how on earth do you
know at this stage of our relationship
which of us is going to get involved?
(PAUSE) So he said he was sorry but
he was just plain scared of any
serious, meaningful relationship.

Example of a draft camera script as it is passed from director to PA.

The front page of the camera script should be set out according to past precedent. It will usually contain the programme number, the title, the author and a list of production and technical staff.

It will also contain the recording date(s), editing and dubbing dates (if known), together with a studio schedule.

Studio schedule

If there is not room on the front page of the camera script for the schedule it should be typed on the second page. The schedule is worked out by the floor manager in consultation with the studio supervisor.

Example:

TUESDAY 27 AUGUST 1986

1100–1300 Camera rehearsal
1300–1400 Lunch
1400–1530 Camera rehearsal
1530–1600 Line up (tea trolley ordered 1530)
1600–1800 Rehearse/RECORD
1800–1900 Supper
1900–2200 Rehearse/RECORD

Technical facilities

Another page will contain the technical facilities: the VTR channels and times booked, the cameras and any special facilities. This information can be obtained from the technical requirements memorandum typed after the planning meeting.

Cast list

There should be a page containing the cast list together with a list of dressing rooms allocated to the artists.

Photographer

If a photographer has been booked, his/her name, telephone number, the times he/she will be on the set and the artists required for a photo-call should be given.

Audience

The arrival time of the audience, if any, should be shown, together with their approximate numbers.

Studio recording order

Then we come to the pages which show the scenes listed in the order in which they are to be recorded. As you will see from the example below the columns denote the following:

Page No.	Shot Nos.	Ep/Scene/Set/Characters	Cam/Sound/Sp. reqs.	Synopsis/time of day
1-8 (4)	1-7	1.3 DINING ROOM, MANNERS HOUSE ALICE JOHN JAMES WILCOX MARY WILCOX ELWYN BRAND GRANT TYLER SARAH GLYN 2 waiters	1A/B/C A1/2 2A/B B1 SWINGER OPEN	Dinner party. Alice finds out about Tew & is regarded with suspicion by James. EVENING.
9-12 (24)	45-46	1.15 DINING ROOM ALICE JOHN	1C 2A 2B B1 SWINGER CLOSED	John accuses Alice of the robbery. MORNING
13-18 (61)	47-60	3.25 DINING ROOM SARAH GLYN JOHN ELWYN GRANT MARY WILCOX JAMES WILCOX DET. INSP. LANDER 2 PCs / 2 waiters	1A/B/C A1/2 2A/B B1 3A/B SWINGER OPEN	Det. Insp. and PCs interrupt dinner party to arrest John. EVENING.
		RECORDING BREAK	/T TO D/2 TO C/	/COSTUME CHANGE JOHN/

Example of a studio recording order.

1. Script page numbers. Both the page number in *recording order* and the page numbers in their original *story order* are given (the story order page numbers are the ones in brackets).
2. Shot numbers. Each shot is numbered consecutively in the camera script. These numbers should be listed in the studio recording order.
3. Episode, scene, set and characters are listed next.
4. Camera/sound/special requirements. The information relevant to this column can be obtained from the director's camera script.
5. Synopsis/time of day. If there is room it is a good idea to include the brief synopsis of the scene which you put in the script breakdown.

Any recording breaks, camera moves, changes in sets, costume and make-up changes should be noted on the recording order. This information can be obtained from the camera script.

A draft recording order is often required for the technical run, but unless the camera script has been finalized before the run, the definitive recording order might contain a number of changes. This final recording order which is to be included in with the camera script is better typed *after* you have both typed and checked the main body of the script. There will be less likelihood of error that way.

The studio recording order is really an annotated form of the camera script. Many of the studio staff work solely from these sheets and additional copies should be made. They should be duplicated in a distinctive colour so that they stand out from the camera script.

The camera script: the body of the document

Now we turn to the main portion of the camera script and the following general guidelines might be helpful:

Colour

The camera script is normally duplicated or photocopied on to yellow paper which allows the type to be clearly read in the studio yet remains distinctive. But if scenes from a number of different episodes are to be shot on the same studio day then each episode may be clearly identified by being duplicated on different coloured paper.

Numbering

The script is typed out and stapled together in *recording* and *not* in *story* order. This means that fresh consecutive page numbers have to be typed or handwritten on the top right hand corner of each page.

Spacing

Sometimes the PA uses the rehearsal script and just types on the camera details, but more often than not she finds that it is quicker to retype the whole document. It is very important not to cram too much information on to a page.

Word processor

It is here, of course, that a specially programmed word processor would prove invaluable by enabling the PA to edit the rehearsal script, add the camera and sound details and alter the layout as necessary.

Consistency of style

Although the layout of the camera script is pretty firmly established, there is plenty of scope for the PA's own, individual style to emerge. Whatever the style, however, it should remain consistent throughout the document.

Boxes

Any technical instructions should be typed inside boxes to make them stand out from the rest of the script. These instructions can refer to cameras, to sound, to lighting, to props, costume, make-up, etc. For example:

/CHANGE CAP/	A note for the capgen operator
/STRIKE ARMCHAIR/	A note for the stage manager
/4 TO C/	A note for camera 4 to move to position C
/FADE UP GRAMS/	A note for the grams operator
/LIGHTING Q/	A note for the lighting director
/QUICK COSTUME CHANGE: ANN/	A note for the costume supervisor

```
(on 35 on 4)                    /WALL B OUT/

                                2A/3C/4E                        B2/C3
                                SCENE 45 : INT. ROOM. NIGHT

        36  2A                  JOHN IS ALONE. IT IS VERY       GRAMS
            W/A ROOM            DARK.  SUDDENLY HIS FACE IS     CAR F/X
                                LIT  BY THE LIGHTS OF A
            SLOW TRACK ROUND    CAR PASSING IN THE STREET
            TO MS JOHN          BELOW/
            /LIGHTING Q/
        37  3C                  / JOHN HALF RISES/
            CU JOHN. HE HALF RISES
        38  4E                  / DET. INSP. (IN DOORWAY)  The
            MS DET. INSP. IN DOORWAY  place is surrounded John.
        39  3C                  You haven't a chance./
            CU JOHN
            MIX                 JOHN   All right.  You win.
        40  4 E                 You always do, don't you./
            MS DET. INSP.


            /FLOATER IN/    Recording break      2 to B   3 to D
```

Example of a camera script that is far too cramped, incorrectly typed and contains inconsistencies of style.

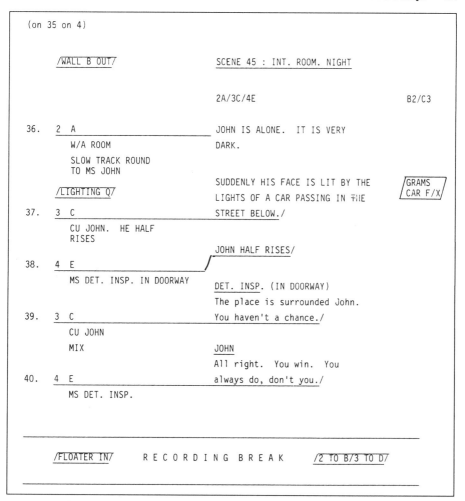

(on 35 on 4)

/WALL B OUT/   SCENE 45 : INT. ROOM. NIGHT

                               2A/3C/4E   B2/C3

36.   2 A   JOHN IS ALONE. IT IS VERY
      W/A ROOM   DARK.
      SLOW TRACK ROUND
      TO MS JOHN
                               SUDDENLY HIS FACE IS LIT BY THE   /GRAMS /
      /LIGHTING Q/   LIGHTS OF A CAR PASSING IN THE   /CAR F/X/
37.   3 C   STREET BELOW./
      CU JOHN. HE HALF
      RISES
                               JOHN HALF RISES/
38.   4 E
      MS DET. INSP. IN DOORWAY DET. INSP. (IN DOORWAY)
                               The place is surrounded John.
39.   3 C   You haven't a chance./
      CU JOHN
      MIX   JOHN
                               All right. You win. You
40.   4 E   always do, don't you./
      MS DET. INSP.

/FLOATER IN/   R E C O R D I N G   B R E A K   /2 TO B/3 TO D/

The same piece, properly typed and correctly spaced.

Top and bottom of page

At the top and bottom of each page the PA should give the preceding and suc-
ceeding shot number and camera. This will assist her in shot calling, of which
more later. For example:

(35 on 4)   At top of page
(43 on 1 next)   At bottom of page

Scenes

As with the rehearsal script, each scene should be started on a fresh page, the dialogue and stage directions typed on the right hand side – allowing sufficient space
on the extreme right for sound instructions – and the pages should be typed single
sided only.

Left hand side

Shot number

The shot number is typed on the extreme left hand side of the page. Every cut is a different shot and should be given a shot number. The numbers should run consecutively in recording order starting from Shot 1. The director might or might not have numbered his shots when drafting the camera script. If he has they should be checked by the PA when typing the script as it is all too easy to miss one out, and if he has not numbered the shots then the PA should do so.

If the camera script is given to the PA in sections, a few scenes at a time as rehearsals progress, she should leave out the shot numbers until she has the complete script.

Camera numbers

Cameras are numbered from one to however many are employed on the production. The director will write which number camera he has chosen for each shot. When the PA is typing the script she should check that the director has not written down two consecutive shots using the same camera or that he has used a camera which is not involved in a particular set. She can do this by having a copy of the floor plan to hand.

At every stage of typing the camera script the PA should check for mistakes. This does not mean that she feels her director is in any way a fool but it is terribly easy to make a slip when writing out a camera script, especially if the director is conducting rehearsals at the same time. If the script does contain any irregularities the PA *must* point them out to the director.

Camera positions

After the number of the camera comes the position it is allocated on the studio floor. This is referred to by letter and corresponds with similar letters on the studio floor plan.

Camera 1 will start in position A then move to position B and end up at position C. On the script it should be typed as 1A, 1B and so on. The PA must check that the director has allowed time for the camera to change position and as a reminder she should type the move as a box on the script, i.e. 1 to B.

Cut line

Directly beneath the camera and its position comes the cut line. This should be typed right across the page and end with a slash upwards at precisely the point at which the director wishes the vision mixer to cut from one shot to another. It should always come at the *end* of the preceding word of dialogue rather than just *before* the new line.

Shot descriptions

Having given each shot a number, a camera and a camera position, the director will then write down a description of the shot he requires. This information should be typed directly under the cut line, in capital letters and inset slightly in order that the camera number is kept clear for the vision mixer to read easily.

```
    CORRECT


                                MAN
 1.   3   A                     That's it then./


                                WOMAN
 2.   1   C                     I told you how it would be./


                                MAN
                                Yes.


    INCORRECT


                                MAN
                                That's it then.


 1.   3   A          / WOMAN
                                I told you how it would be.


 2.   1   C          / MAN
                                Yes.
```

Example of correct and incorrect cut lines. Even if the director has drafted his camera script with the cut line before the new line rather than at the end of the old, the PA should type out the camera script correctly.

A list of commonly used shot descriptions and abbreviations is given on page 123.

If the shot develops then the further camera instructions should be typed as near as possible against the relevant line of dialogue or stage directions.

Recording break

A recording break signifies that the recording will be stopped. This could be for any one of a number of reasons: to allow a camera to move position; to shift an article of furniture; to move a wall of a set; a costume change, etc., etc.

In a rehearse/record situation where a scene or number of consecutive scenes are rehearsed and then recorded before going on to rehearse the next block (as opposed to a rehearsal of the whole of the programme followed by a recording) the

(50 on 4)   - 35 -

                                             SCENE 10

                                             INT. DAY. OFFICE

                                             CAMS 1B/C 2A/B   B1 A2

51 1 B   SUE IS SITTING AT AN OFFICE DESK.
        WS. SUE L FRAME   LESLEY IS PACING UP AND DOWN.
        LESLEY R

                                             LESLEY

        CRAB L. HOLD &   Well I said to him - you can't have
        TIGHTEN TO MS LESLEY
                                             it both ways Trevor - you've got to

                                             get your priorities straight my lad

                                             - either we have a serious, meaningful

52 2 A   relationship/or I don't want to know.
        MS SUE

                                             SUE

53 1 B   What did he say?/
        MS LESLEY

                                             LESLEY

                                             He said he didn't want to get involved.

54 2 A   I mean, honestly! /
        MS SUE

                                             SUE

55 1 B   So what did you say?/
        MS LESLEY

        HOLD HER AS SHE SITS   LESLEY (SITTING DOWN)

                                             Well I said - how on earth do you

                                             know at this stage of our relationship

                                             which of us is going to get involved?

        .TIGHTEN TO. MCU   (PAUSE) So he said he was sorry but

                                             he was just plain scared of any

                                             serious, meaningful relationship.

(2 next)

Example of positioning of shot descriptions.

recording break might occur to allow the next scene or scenes to be rehearsed through.

If a break is indicated it should be marked on the camera script by drawing two lines straight across the page. Any technical instructions should be typed in the centre.

Example:

RECORDING BREAK

/5 to H/3 to K/   /STRIKE G'FATHER CLOCK/   /COSTUME CHANGE:

MARTIN/JILL/FIONA/

Film or VTR inserts

Film or VTR inserts should likewise be isolated from the main body of the script by means of drawing two lines across the page. They will then stand out more clearly.

'As directed' sequences

If part of the programme is fully scripted and part 'as directed', lines should be drawn across the page for the 'as directed' sequences. Type in the cameras allocated at the top and leave plenty of space for shots and notes to be inserted during rehearsal.

Right hand side

The right hand side of the page of camera script contains all the dialogue and sound details (see example on p. 122):

1. Top of scene

Directly under the scene heading should be typed a list of the characters appearing in that scene, the cameras and their positions. On the extreme right hand side the booms (microphones extended on long poles) should be noted.

2. Booms

Each boom is identified by letter and its position on the set by number, thus avoiding confusion with the cameras. Therefore the booms involved in a set might be A1, B2 and so on.

3. Dialogue

Then follows the dialogue and stage directions of the scene set out as for the rehearsal script but intersected by cut lines. Don't forget that it is far better and quicker in the long run to retype the page or pages rather than try to fit all the camera and sound instructions around the original text. Don't be afraid of spreading the script so that everything is comfortably spaced.

SCENE 2 : DAY. INT. TOWER

LADY ANN/LORD GREY/JAILER

1K, 2C, 3A   B1, A2

IT IS LATE MORNING AND ANN   /GRAMS: BELL/
IS SITTING SEWING. A BELL
TOLLS IN THE DISTANCE.

THE DOOR OPENS AND LORD GREY
ENTERS WITH THE JAILER.

JAILOR
It's strictly against orders
my Lord.

LORD GREY DOES NOT REACT

It could cost me my job - let
alone my head...

LORD GREY
All right man. (HE HANDS HIM
SOME MONEY) Take yourself off.

JAILER
Thank you my Lord. (HE GOES)

THE BELL CEASES. SILENCE.
THEN A SINGLE GUN SHOT IS HEARD   /F/X: GUN/

Example of typed out camera script.

4. *Sound information*

On the extreme right hand side of the page comes any sound information, for example:

☐ Spot effects (f/x), performed by the assistant stage manager in the studio on cue from the director, e.g. door slam, footsteps.
☐ Effects on record (grams) or tape, e.g. bells ringing, clocks ticking, hoofbeats.
☐ Background atmosphere (atmos.) e.g. birdsong, traffic and so on.
☐ Music played into the studio from grams or tape.

Much of the sound nowadays is built up in the post production stage during the sound dub, but there are still certain effects which need to be recorded at the time.

If the sound is to continue for a specific time, a line should be drawn down the side of the page to denote the duration.

Camera script terms

The following gives a list of the most commonly used shot descriptions and abbreviations:

Shot descriptions

W/A	Wide angle shot. Such a shot takes place in a wide area of the set in front of the camera. It is sometimes referred to as a VLS (very long shot).
LS	Long shot. A shot which directs the viewer's eye to the depth rather than the width of the shot.
MLS	Medium long shot. Refers to a shot comprising the head to just below the knee of the subject.
3–s	Three shot. A shot containing three central characters.
2–s	Two shot. A shot containing two central characters.
2–s fav. X	A shot with two people - the camera favours one person more than the other.
o/s 2–s	Over the shoulder two shot. Two people are seen in the shot but the camera is looking at one of them over the shoulder of the other.
Mid 2–s	Comprising the head to just below the waist of two people.
Close 2–s	Comprising the head and shoulders of two people.
MS	Mid shot. A scene at normal viewing distance. In the case of a human subject the camera frame cuts the figure just below the waist.
MCU	Medium close up. The camera frame cuts the figure at chest level.
CU	Close up. The camera frame cuts the subject just below the neck.
BCU	Big close up. The face fills the frame.
X's POV	X's point of view shot. The camera is X and sees as if from his point of view.
H/A	High angle. The camera is above the action and looking down on it.
L/A	Low angle. The camera is below the action and looking up.

Camera movements

Panning	Camera turns from one side to the other, pivoting horizontally on an axis, either right to left or left to right.
Tilting	Camera pivoting vertically on an axis, tilting up or down.
Tracking	Camera is physically moved forward or back, towards or away from the subject.
Crabbing	The camera is physically moved crab-wise or sideways to the direction of view.
Craning and jibbing	A movement by a camera mounted on a crane dolly. The dolly has a jib arm which can be raised and lowered rotating around its fulcrum.
Z/I	Zoom in. The camera is not moved but the focal length of the zoom lens is increased. This magnifies the subject without changing the perspective of the scene (as opposed to a track where the camera moves towards the subject and the perspective changes as if you were walking towards it).
Z/O	Zoom out. The lens is adjusted in the reverse direction from the above.

Abbreviations relating to action

A/B	As before
FAV	Favouring
F/G	Foreground
B/G	Background
F/WD	Forward
B/WD	Backward
X's	Crosses or across
CAM R	Camera right, i.e. as seen from the camera's – and the viewer's – position when facing the action
CAM L	Camera left
O/S	Over the shoulder
OOV	Out of vision
OOFL(R)	Out of frame left (or right)
Q	Cue
S/B	Stand by

Abbreviations relating to sound

F/U	Fade up
F/D	Fade down
MUTE	Without sound
V/O	Voice over
S.O.F	Sound on film
S.O.T	Sound on tape
S.O.VT	Sound on videotape
S & V	Sound and vision
MIC	Microphone

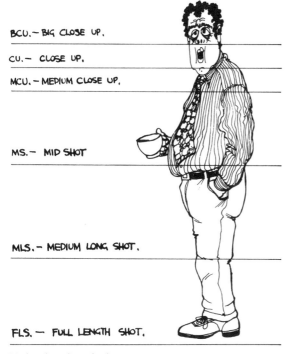

BCU. – BIG CLOSE UP.

CU. – CLOSE UP.

MCU. – MEDIUM CLOSE UP.

MS. – MID SHOT

MLS. – MEDIUM LONG SHOT.

FLS. – FULL LENGTH SHOT.

Main shot descriptions.

GRAMS   Music or sound effects from gramophone records. It is also used as an instruction to the person known as the 'grams operator', therefore could also refer to music or sound effects on tape.

TAPE   Music or sound effects solely from tape recordings

F/X   Effects

SPOT F/X   Sound effects made in the studio

ATMOS   Atmosphere

Instructions for vision mixer

F/O   Fade out

T/O   Take out

S/I   Superimpose

WIPE

MIX

CUT

Abbreviations relating to graphics or computer effects

DFS or DVE Digital frame store or digital video effects

CK   Chromakey. Replacing part of an electronic picture with material from another source. In some companies this is known as **CSO** (colour separation overlay).

B/E   Black edge generator. The outlining of letters on screen to help
                      legibility.
CPU   Caption projection unit.

Camera cards

Once the camera script has been typed and checked it should be photocopied or
duplicated and made available to everyone on the production who needs it. The
cast would not need copies of the camera script.

The PA prepares camera cards for the camera operators. These are ideally typed
on thin card or on paper which is stapled to cards. The typing should be clear
enough for reading under possibly dim lighting conditions. Don't type the cards
using a faint, worn-out ribbon!

Each card contains only the information relevant to that particular camera:
camera 1 would receive cards with the minimum details of camera 1's shots and so
on. The shots are extracted by the PA from the main body of the camera script.

Type on the card the shot numbers relevant to that camera, the camera's position and a description of the shot. Do keep the description brief and unambiguous,
no matter how your director has phrased it on the camera script. For example:

On camera script:

START TIGHT ON HARRY, FRAMING HIS HEAD AND SHOULDERS.
WIDEN SHOT AS HE WALKS R TO DRINKS CABINET AND PAN WITH
HIM.

Should read on camera card:

MCU HARRY
WIDEN & PAN HIM R (TO DRINKS CABINET)

Keep it brief and concise.

Every episode, scene and set should be marked on the camera card as well as the
numbers of the other cameras operating during that scene. Recording breaks, tape
run-ons, film and VTR inserts should also be included on the cards of all the cameras involved.

The typing *must* be well spaced out. Don't type too much on a card and don't put
a fast shot change at the bottom of a card. It is far better to leave half a card blank
if necessary.

Do leave plenty of room on the right hand side of the card as well as underneath
each shot for notes to be added. This is especially important when 'as directed'
sequences are involved.

Distribution and use

The PA should give the sets of cards to the camera operators. Cameras with more
than one operator, i.e. cameras on dollies or cranes, will need additional sets of
cards.

During the studio the camera operators will be listening to the PA calling the
shots (see Chapter 8) and will have a clear reference on their cards as to the point

that has been reached in the script – by virtue of the shot number called – the number and description of the shot for which they will next be required and the position to which they should move.

It is also useful to remind camera operators more than once of the shot they are on and what is coming next during shots of lengthy duration.

CAMERA : One		Page 3	TITLE : JOE AND HARRY
Shot	Pos.	Description	Notes
		SCENE 2 : DAY. INT. HALL	
		(CAMS 1A/B, 2C, 3A)	
9	A	2-s JOE/MARY	
		TRACK WITH JOE AS HE	
		X'S L. LOSE MARY	
		Then TOTON WITH MOVE	
		GRAB LEFT TO MISS SETTEE	
14	A	MS JOE *(AS HE TURNS)*	
14 B		*A/B (HE TURNS AWAY)*	
		/T TO B/	
24	B	DEEP 3-s FAV. JOE	
		PAN JOE R & TIGHTEN	
		INTO 2-s. JOE SITS. *(WATCH IT HE SITS FAST !)*	
		RECORDING BREAK	

Example of a camera card.

8

The recording

The great day has at last arrived – the day which, unlike the PAs on live shows, you might have spent months working towards – the day of the studio.

In an earlier chapter I wrote that the PA on a live programme takes surprisingly little into the studio gallery. This is not unfortunately true of recorded programmes. For those you must prepare to virtually transport your entire production office – to decamp as it were from your comfortable surroundings and set up home in the confined space of the studio gallery. Just take comfort in the thought that it is far far worse on location! So – what you should take?

What to take

Camera scripts

If there has not been time to distribute these in advance then you must do so as first priority on the morning of the studio.

You should give copies to those in the gallery – the vision mixer, the studio supervisor, the capgen operator (if you have one). Copies should be left in the sound and lighting control areas.

You should leave copies at strategic points on the studio floor, give a copy to VTR where the programme is to be recorded and, if film inserts are to be played in, a copy should be left with telecine. Leave copies in the Operations Room. Any remaining copies should be kept with you in case of need.

Recording orders

Spare recording orders should be left on the floor of the studio and in the gallery.

Studio call sheets

Should be typed up with the artists' names then given to the stage manager who will fill in the call times.

Rehearsal scripts

You might like to take a few copies of the rehearsal script to the studio.

Camera cards

These are to be distributed to the camera operators first thing.

Programme file

Despite its weight you might find it useful to take with you to the studio. If you leave it in the office you will undoubtedly need it.

Address and telephone list

Anyone in any way connected with the production should be included in your address and telephone list and you should take it to the studio.

Key personnel in the building

A telephone list of the key people in the building, i.e. reception, canteen, security, etc. should be to hand.

Time chart

You should either take your own rehearsal script with the written-in timings taken from the final rehearsal, or have a time chart made out with these timings for each individual scene, a column for cumulative timings and several blank columns.

Records/tapes

You should ensure that any music needed for the studio is taken to the sound control areas. Likewise any sound effects on disc or tape, although these will probably have been acquired by the sound supervisor.

Captions/graphics/transparencies

If any graphics are to be recorded you must make sure they are taken to the studio and given to the correct person. Many productions nowadays will, however, insert titles, credits and any graphics during the post production stage.

Stopwatch(es)

Make sure you have one (or more) with you and that it is in good working order.

Pencils/coloured pens/erasers/ruler

All necessary office equipment should be taken to the gallery, including pencil sharpener, hole puncher, stapler, paperclips and scissors.

Blank and ruled paper

Take sufficient with you for taking down notes from the director and notes for editing.

'Just take comfort in the thought that it is far far worse on location.'

Throat pastilles

You can get quite hoarse after a twelve hour studio so take some soothing throat sweets.

And finally most PAs carry a selection of the following at the bottom of their seemingly bottomless bags - aspirins, indigestion tablets, tissues, safety pins . . . the list can be endless.

The studio floor

You arrive in the gallery at an early hour, deposit your travelling office on the desk and settle down to . . .

Not quite yet. Before making yourself comfortable in the gallery you must go round distributing camera cards, running orders, scripts, records, captions and so on.

Eyeball-to-eyeball contact

And in so doing you should get to know the people involved in your production. For the rest of the day - or days - you and they will be simply disembodied voices. It is far better for you to meet face to face. It will make for a better working atmosphere and you will not have time later on.

Some camera operators have commented that many PAs seem scared of going down on to the studio floor. They act as if they are trespassing and approach people in a furtive manner, heads down, silently handing over the camera cards before scuttling back to the relative security of the gallery. It is unclear whether this is due to an inbuilt and unfounded sense of superiority or, more likely, a strong sense of inferiority, of feeling that one knows one's place as PA and that place is *not* on the floor of the studio. However, camera operators are known to be human and, like everyone else, they want a PA to whom they can relate, a real person as opposed to a voice.

So do go down to the floor of the studio, walk round the sets - taking care of course not to get in the way - find out the names of the camera operators and boom swingers and become aware that you belong here as well as in the gallery.

To help you do this, let us wander round the floor of our fictitious drama.

The sets

These will have been constructed overnight in all probability. Their design will not be entirely unfamiliar to you as you will have seen the scale model and floor plan and watched the final rehearsals. However it will look different from your own conception if only because of the addition of props and furnishings.

The designer, the stage manager and a host of stage hands will be busy on the sets, adding the final touches and sorting out any last minute problems.

Lighting

The lights will be high above you, bank upon bank of them. Electricians will be positioning them and they will be controlled by the lighting control area adjacent to the main gallery.

Cameras

Studio cameras are fairly large and give high quality pictures. Their lenses are top quality, generally zoom lenses able to give shots of differing size. They are fitted on to different sorts of mountings according to the needs of the production. Full communication is standard enabling talkback to and from the director and PA.

There are, in addition, a range of lightweight cameras which are used extensively on single camera outside broadcasts. Their use in a studio situation may be more limited.

Camera mountings

Pedestals (peds) are the bread-and-butter of most studio productions. The cameras are mounted on the pedestals which gives them a great amount of stability. The

'So go down to the floor of the studio, walk around the sets – taking care not to get in the way . . .'

pedestals are on wheels so they can be used for crabbing and tracking shots. They are extremely versatile since they can also vary the height of the camera.

A dolly is a mounting designed to carry out specific movements. For example there is:

- [ ] A crane dolly, which is a mobile camera mounting with a jib arm that can be raised and lowered to a greater degree than the pedestal.
- [ ] A crab dolly is a type of mounting which can be moved sideways as well as forward.
- [ ] A high angle dolly is a crane in an elevated position which can achieve high shots. Sometimes the camera operator is seated with his camera but on certain mountings the camera operator is remote from his camera. This particular mounting has incredible flexibility but takes additional skill in use.
- [ ] A low angle dolly is a mounting used to give low shots. In using a low angle dolly however the director could easily shoot over the top of the set.

Cranes can be used very effectively in a production but they can be limiting because they take up a lot of space, need time to be manoeuvred into position and require additional personnel to man them. A lightweight camera placed on a mini-crane is more flexible in that respect.

On a fairly typical drama production there might be four, possibly five, pedestal cameras with perhaps one lightweight camera. A dolly might be used on some, but not all, of the studio days.

Sound

Microphones would be placed at the positions laid down in the studio floor plan. They are held in place over the sets by means of booms, which are telescopic arms. Each boom has its individual operator.

Gallery duties

If you feel that you are only allowed in the studio on sufferance then your return to the gallery will be like a home-coming. But this security will only be truly felt after your belongings have been spread out to your satisfaction and your base established.

Every PA will have her own precise, rigid way of setting out her script, blank paper, ruler, pens, pencils, stopwatches and so on. She will arrange them in a pattern most pleasing to herself and for her greatest comfort and accessibility. She needs to be reassured in advance that if she stretches out her hand for a stopwatch, a pencil, a ruler, that object will be waiting at the precise spot without her having to hunt for it on the desk.

Camera rehearsal

The first thing that happens in a programme that is to be recorded is a rehearsal with cameras, otherwise know as the 'stagger through'. The director will rehearse one scene, or a section of that scene or a whole piece of the script with the actors and will talk the camera operators through the shots he wants. This rehearsal might go on for a morning, a whole day or, if the production is to be rehearse/ record there might only be a short rehearsal before recording.

Some directors conduct the rehearsals totally from the gallery, some conduct them from the floor of the studio. If the director takes the rehearsals from the floor you should remain in the gallery to act as general liaison in addition to calling the shots.

Note taking

The director might expect you to take notes throughout the rehearsal for anyone involved in the production but for whom he does not wish, at that moment, to interrupt the rehearsal. Most notes will be given as muttered asides and sometimes you will not be sure whether you are meant to write them down. Do note down everything.

Group the notes under headings, i.e. notes for artists, notes for sound and so on as this will save time later when the director gives them out.

If the director has been rehearsing from the gallery he will usually go down to the studio floor once the rehearsal is over. You will accompany him armed with the notes. Either you will be asked to give them directly to people or, more likely, you will be asked to remind him of the points he wishes to raise.

If you have been using shorthand to take down the notes do make sure that you can read them back quickly and accurately.

Answering queries

During the rehearsal there will be a lot of queries arising from all areas concerning, for example, equipment that has not arrived, organizational matters that need attending to, anything and everything. Deal with the matters you know about yourself and pass others on to the right person. Part of your job is to act as a sorting house, routing queries in the right direction.

Answering the telephone

If the telephone needs answering it will not ring but a white light will flash. You should answer it during rehearsals, unless you are otherwise engaged when the studio supervisor will answer it. You will know whether or not the call is urgent. Don't, for example, interrupt the rehearsal to tell the actor Fred Bloggs that his cleaning lady forgot to collect the vacuum cleaner from the repairers and therefore his house will remain dirty. You can tell him later. If agents ring, generally you can pass the message on at a convenient break in rehearsal. Just use your intelligence.

Script changes

You should mark any script changes that occur as rehearsals progress whether these changes are in the dialogue or concerning the cameras. As the director sees the shots he will undoubtedly wish to make revisions to the script, to add shots, develop shots, change camera positions and so on. You must ensure that everyone is aware of these changes, if necessary by talking them through the script at the end of rehearsal and prior to recording.

Throughout the studio your script will probably get messy as things change for a second and even third time. You might well be tempted to mark up a fresh script

Changes to a camera script.

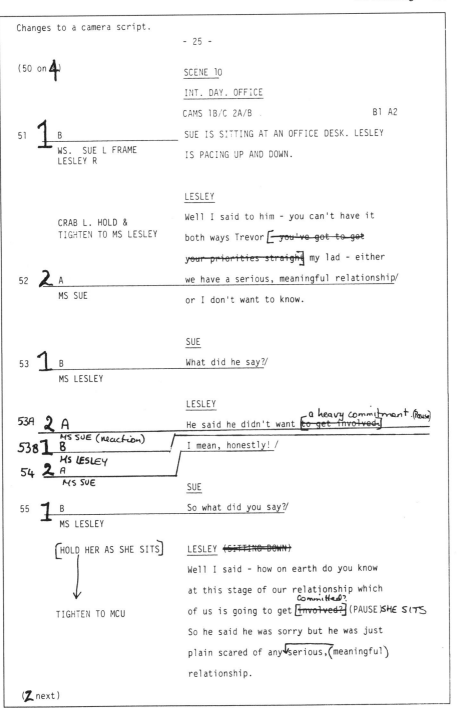

- 25 -

(50 on 4)

SCENE 10

INT. DAY. OFFICE

CAMS 1B/C 2A/B .   B1 A2

51 1 B   SUE IS SITTING AT AN OFFICE DESK. LESLEY
    WS. SUE L FRAME   IS PACING UP AND DOWN.
    LESLEY R

                                LESLEY

    CRAB L. HOLD &   Well I said to him - you can't have it
    TIGHTEN TO MS LESLEY   both ways Trevor [you've got to get

                                your priorities straight] my lad - either

52 2 A   we have a serious, meaningful relationship/
    MS SUE   or I don't want to know.

                                SUE

53 1 B   What did he say?/
    MS LESLEY

                                LESLEY   a heavy commitment.(Pause)
53A 2 A   He said he didn't want [to get involved.]
    MS SUE (reaction)
53B 1 B   / I mean, honestly! /
    MS LESLEY
54 2 A
    MS SUE

                                SUE

55 1 B   So what did you say?/
    MS LESLEY

    [HOLD HER AS SHE SITS]   LESLEY (SITTING DOWN)

                                Well I said - how on earth do you know

                                at this stage of our relationship which
                                              Committed?
    TIGHTEN TO MCU   of us is going to get [involved?] (PAUSE) SHE SITS

                                So he said he was sorry but he was just

                                plain scared of any serious, (meaningful)

                                relationship.

(2 next)

Example of changes to a camera script.

just before the recording. If you do you will almost certainly leave out some vital alteration or instruction. So don't do it! It is far better for you to take plenty of erasers and rub out unwanted instructions as you work through the rehearsals.

Just before the recording you might find it helpful to mark the cameras in large red figures down your script. This will be an aid to you when shot calling, which we will be looking at next.

Shot calling and timing

We have already looked at the role of the PA as the central point of communications, both in the setting up and during the recording or transmission of a programme.

As part of this, one of the main duties of the PA when working in the control gallery of a studio is to keep everyone informed verbally of what is happening at that moment and what is to come next. It is an important task because most of the technical people on the production will have neither the time nor the facility for keeping their eyes on the script or running order. If there is no script the importance of this job is self-evident.

On a live, news-type programme we have already seen that the PA will perform this function partly by talking the studio through the running order, partly by

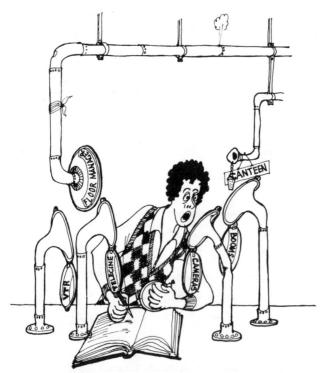

'One of the main duties of the PA when working in the control gallery of a studio is to keep everyone informed verbally of what is happening . . .'

counting through the items and partly by keeping the studio constantly informed as to how much time is left.

On an unscripted outside broadcast which is dictated by the events that are being transmitted, the PA provides an essential commentary on what is happening now and what is about to happen by means of 'living in the future'.

On a scripted programme, whether live or recorded, the PA performs the same task in a very precise and exact fashion by means of shot calling.

It is precise because each different shot has been given a consecutive number either by the director when drafting the script or by the PA when typing it in its finished form. By calling out the number of the shot she keeps the entire studio informed about the place which has been reached in the script.

Warning for camera operators

In addition to calling out the shot, the PA should also give the camera operators a warning of which camera is to be used next. It must be remembered that the camera operators work from the list of shots relating to their own camera as written on their camera cards. They do not usually work from the full camera script therefore they rely very much on the PA giving them warning standbys.

What to say

As in almost everything in television, there is no standardized method of shot calling. At least two systems are currently in use in the UK: there might be more.

1. The first system of shot calling is to call the number of the shot that is currently being shown on the transmission monitor and the number of the camera which the vision mixer will cut to next.

   For example: 'Shot 40, 2 next' - meaning that we are currently recording or transmitting shot number 40 and the next shot will be on camera 2. '41, 1 next, 42, 2 next, 43, 4 next' and so on.

2. In the second system of shot calling the PA does not call out the number of the shot that is currently being transmitted or recorded but calls out both the shot number and camera that will come next.

   For example: 'Shot 41 on 2 next' - meaning that the next shot will be number 41 on camera 2 (the understanding being that we are currently on shot 40), '42 on 1 next, 43 on 2 next, 44 on 4 next' and so on.

I cannot say, as I have tried to do throughout this book, that both systems have their advantages. My feeling is that the first system is far better both for the PA who is calling the shots and for those at the other end of the communications system who are listening.

My reasons are:

(a) The second method does not fulfil the requirement of telling everyone what is happening *at that moment* as well as what is to happen next, and it must be remembered that camera operators are not the only people who are listening to the PA. Some of the recipients are more interested in the current shot and are not necessarily interested in the one that is to come next.

(b) By using the second method the PA is working one step ahead of everyone else and it would be relatively easy for her to get confused and start calling the wrong shots. That, for everyone concerned, is far worse than not calling any shots at all.

(c) On a fast shot calling sequence, the PA using the first method drops the advance warning to camera operators and concentrates on the actual shot that has been punched up on the transmission monitor, i.e. '41, 42, 43, 44' and so on. But if the second method were used the PA would have to add the word 'next' to every single shot she called, i.e. '41 next, 42 next' and so on. While this may seem trivial to anyone who has not had to conduct a fast shot calling sequence, believe me that 'next' would matter and could make it difficult for the PA to keep up with the shot changes.

Having said all that, however, the individual PA will have to use whatever method is employed in the company for whom she works.

The big trap

The biggest trap the PA can fall into when shot calling – whatever method she and her company favour – is one mentioned earlier in the book, that of *not watching the monitors.*

It is the easiest trap in the world to fall into and we have all done it, especially when confronted by a complicated sequence with a large number of shots. You look at your script, listen to the dialogue and call the shots according to the director's instructions. But if you do that you will be very likely to go wrong and once you have gone wrong, unless you check the monitor and rectify your mistake, you will continue to call the wrong shots throughout the sequence.

By being inaccurate in shot calling you could easily confuse the camera operators as well as everyone else listening to you. However, everyone would soon realise that you were unreliable and would cease to listen. You *must* be accurate or not speak at all. And you can *only* ensure continuing accuracy if you keep your head up and watch the transmission monitor. It is only after the shot has been punched up on the screen that you should speak.

You might find it helpful to hold your script up on a level with the monitors so that your eyes can flick comfortably from one to the other rather than having to raise and lower your head each time you call a shot.

Previewing

In addition to calling the shots, and as part of the operation, you must keep an eye on the shot that is to come next. If the camera operator is not ready with the required shot you might need to give him a further reminder, i.e. 'Coming to *you* next, 2'.

Other 'do's'

Do speak clearly and concisely. This applies to anything you say over studio talkback, but a PA who mumbles when shot calling will only result in people either not listening at all or irritably asking you to speak up.

During a long shot on one camera do remind everyone what is happening, i.e. 'still on shot 51 on 5' and issue a further warning to the next camera operator near the end of the shot, i.e. 'coming to 2'.

Keep the studio informed whatever is happening next. If it is to be a recording break, a film or VTR insert, a tape run-on (i.e. the recording continues) while a camera is re-positioned, let everyone know.

The director and vision mixer will normally remind camera operators of moves, but if they do not then you should. For example, if, during a sequence intercutting between cameras 1 and 2 (shots 31-40), camera 3 is required to move to position B to be ready for shot 41, just ensure that camera 3 *has* moved and *is* in position. It is a bit late to warn him if you have already reached shot 40 without him moving.

Apart from shot calling, if you wish to warn the camera operator about a move or a change or communicate in any way, do be polite about it and do not shout instructions.

If the camera operator wishes to communicate with the gallery he might well move his camera vigorously from side to side or up and down. If you see this movement before the director, tell the director.

'If you wish to warn the camera operator about a move or a change or communicate in any way, do be polite about it and not shout instructions.'

Timing

If you have read through this book from the beginning, right now you must be sitting on the edge of your seat wondering why on earth I have not yet mentioned timing as a prerequisite among the duties of the PA on a recorded programme. Is it not important?

Yes, timing is important and it does matter. But certain aspects of the PA's job have priority over others, depending upon the type of programme on which you are working; on a programme which is to be recorded and which has ample editing before transmission, timing is not a major consideration.

On a programme which is recorded 'as live' with no editing or only a minimum of editing allowed, or on a programme with very tight turn round and little time for editing, timing becomes more important.

Read-through and final run timings

At the initial read-through and again during the final rehearsal you will have taken timings. Most probably you will have written them on the pages of your rehearsal script, ideally at one minute intervals or at least once on every page of script. The timings will be taken from your stopwatch and you will have added together the durations of each scene until you have an overall timing.

The timings you take at the final rehearsal will be of most use to the director and producer because, as a result of your calculations, scenes might have to be dropped or extensive re-writes done with the aim of cutting down or building up the script before going into the studio.

So, hopefully, you will go into the studio with roughly the right length script for the time slot allocated, or at any rate with a good idea of by how much it is likely to over- or under-run.

The only exception being if you have a number of time-consuming action props that have only been mimed through in rehearsal. Drawing a cork out of a wine bottle for example might only take seconds in rehearsal without the cork, but takes very much longer with the real thing.

I am also writing specifically here about the highly-controlled drama-type recorded programme. Timings on other recorded programmes might require other measures. In variety programmes for example, allowance has to be made for audience reaction.

Timings during the studio

During the camera rehearsals you should get into the habit of taking timings and noting down the durations of scenes. During the recordings you should switch to red or another colour pen and continue to take down the timings.

Some PAs note the timing at the foot of each page of script, while others write it at the top of each page or half-way down. If you note the timing half-way down each page you will be less likely to lose your place in the script as you turn over the page. Whatever you do, however, be consistent.

During the recording you should compare the real times with the rehearsal times in order to see whether the programme is over- or under-running.

Remember that you should only time from the moment the director says 'Cue'.

	SCENE/SET	REH. TIMES	CUM.	STUDIO TIMES	CUM.
1	DAY. EXT. STREET (FILM)	2.10		(F) 2.10	
8	DAY. EXT. CAR PARK (FILM)	3.40	5.50	(F) 3.40	5.50
14	INT. ENTRANCE	.20	6.10	.20	6.10
15	CORRIDOR	1.00	7.10	1.10	7.20
2	KITCHEN	5.10	12.20	5.05	12.25
4	"	2.15	14.35	2.20	14.45
12	"	4.05	18.40		
18	"	1.00	19.40		
13	DINING ROOM	3.05	22.45		
16	"	6.25	29.10		
20	"	6.00	35.10		
3	LOUNGE	2.00	37.10		
5	"	.35	37.45		
7	"	2.10	39.55		
9	"	1.05	41.00		
17	"	4.15	45.15		
19	"	.15	45.30		
6	BEDROOM	3.10	48.40		
10	"	2.50	51.30		
11	HALLWAY	.10	51.40		

Time chart for a 50 minute studio drama. The scenes are listed in *recording* order as otherwise it would be impossible to add up a cumulative running time during the recording.

Time code logging

It has been stated elsewhere in this book that few programmes nowadays are recorded in their final story order. There are many reasons for this, the most important being the complexity of programmes today allied to the vast technological improvements in videotape editing.

As a result we have scenes or sequences recorded in sections, recorded in an order which is determined by the number and type of sets, the facility of camera movements, the availability of artists and so on. On a multi-episodic series, scenes from different episodes will be recorded on the same studio day, i.e. all the scenes set in the kitchen would be shot together.

Film or video inserts are now rarely played directly into the studio but are usually edited in later.

In addition, directors used to the flexibility of the single camera 'film' type technique of shooting, often adapt it as best they can to the multi-camera situation, re-recording scenes shot multi-camera in order to obtain further shots from different angles.

Then again, each section that is recorded might have a number of takes for all sorts of reasons ranging from inadequate performance by the artists to errors of a technical nature, culminating in the director's 'gut' feeling that the scene could be improved by re-taking it.

So we end up after the studio with a mass of unrelated material which must now be reassembled, sorted and edited into correct story order.

It is therefore of prime importance that the PA keeps a note of what is recorded in the order in which it has been shot. She needs to note the number of takes, their duration and the reason why they were not considered usable. To do this she needs some means of identifying the position of each recorded section on the reels of videotape.

In the past she would have done this by using a stopwatch as a means of reference, adding up a cumulative 'tape running' time and noting down her specific times from that. It was not that accurate and could become very complicated. The advent of time code revolutionized the PA's work in this respect by providing an identification which is recorded on every frame of videotape.

What is time code?

Time code was developed in 1967. It is a method whereby each video frame is identified by means of numbers broken down into hours, minutes, seconds and frames. Each frame always keeps its original identity, known as the time code address. This makes logging and editing more precise and efficient.

Time code is normally recorded on an audio track which is then played through a time code reader which produces the relevant numbers. These numbers are often inset in a box, white letters on black, and are displayed on a monitor in the gallery in hours, minutes and seconds (the frames' digits normally being omitted for simplicity). Sometimes there can be a prefix number to identify the different episodes, i.e. 02.02.32.06 would mean Episode 2, two hours, thirty-two minutes, six seconds.

Some studio galleries have a time code reader on the desk which the PA can freeze in order to write down the time. When she cancels the button the time code will revert to the present.

The time code recorded on to the tape can either show the tape running time or the actual time of day. Some companies use one system, some another and some a combination of the two depending upon the programme.

Tape running time

This has the advantage of letting the PA know the position reached on the tape and how much blank tape is left. There is also no possibility of duplication of numbers and tape running time code tends to be preferred by videotape editors as time of day time code can cause problems in editing.

Time of day time code

This system records the actual time of day on the tape. It is most useful on location when the PA is trying to compile a shot list without having access to a monitor with inset time code. She can then take the time from a digital watch.

However when the same tape is used two days running there is the possibility of a duplication of time code numbers on the same reel. Either a fresh reel should be started each day or the PA should note down the date as well as the time code.

TIME CODE SHOWN
IN HOURS, MINUTES AND SECONDS.

Time code logging.

Recording log

The PA should compile an accurate log of the recording by noting down the 'in' points of time code at the start of each section of recording and noting the information given below.

It is not necessary for her to note down the 'out' points of time code at the moment the recording is stopped unless she is not using a stopwatch and needs to work out the running time of each recorded section solely from the time code readouts.

This log is built up during the recording and written out during the studio. It should contain the following:

1. Videotape reel number

This is most important if a number of reels are used during the course of the studio.

2. Time code 'in' point

This should be from the moment the director cues the action in the studio.

3. Shot numbers

Taken from the camera script of the recorded section.

| VTR ROLL 9 | | RECORDING LOG | | | "THE LONG SEARCH" | |
| | | | | | REC: 25 September 1985 | |
"In" t/c	Shot nos.	Ep/Scene	Take	Notes	R/T
01.15.26	69-74	3.24	1	Boom in shot	2.00
01.17.30	"	"	2	OK	2.00
01.19.40	75-85	3.37	1	OK	3.20
01.23.10	86	2.10	1	Action n/g	.30
01.24.00	"	"	2	Cam wobble	.30
01.24.40	"	"	3	Cable in shot	.30
01.25.15	"	"	4	OK	.30
01.25.55	87-100	1.15	1	NG action	4.10
01.30.20	"	"	2	OK	4.05
01.34.30	96-100	"	1	Insert shots - poss	.45
01.35.25	"	"	2	" OK	.45

Example of typed up recording log.

4. Episode and scene numbers

Should be marked on the log, especially if the recording is multi-episodic as it is vital to preface every scene with its correct episode.

5. Take numbers

This should correspond with the verbal ident given by the floor manager.

6. Notes

Anything that was wrong with the recorded section should be noted down and any additional notes or reminders for the editor should be written in this column.

7. Running time

The running time, taken from the stopwatch, should be written down.

These lists could then be typed out after the studio, especially if the director requires a copy for viewing the recorded material before going into editing. If the director does not require a copy and if your notes are legible enough for you to read them don't bother to type them.

Coverage script

By compiling the recording log, you will have noted down exactly what happened during the studio in the order in which it was recorded. If you then attend the editing with this log and work from it by informing the editor of the correct reels and time code points in which to re-assemble the material in its final story order, you might find it difficult and time-wasting as you hunt through your lists of notes in order to find the desired shots in the correct order.

This is where the coverage (or tramline) script is so valuable. The script, which you would mark up in rough on your own camera script during the studio, has the 'in' point of time code and lines down the page covering the length of the recorded sections.

If you have time during the studio, if not afterwards, mark up a clean camera script for the editing.

In this way you will be able to see *in story order* what is required for editing and you will speed up the whole editing operation.

Light entertainment and music

Light entertainment covers a very wide range of programmes: situation comedies, stand-up comedians, quiz shows, music shows, chat shows and so on. The programmes are frequently studio-based but they might be made as an outside broadcast or on film or contain many elements within the same programme. They are often transmitted live or recorded 'as live' in front of an audience. The PA on light entertainment programmes will find herself using the whole range of her technical skills as she moves from one show to another.

Many of the skills she needs will have been discussed earlier in the book, but there are, however, a few points that specifically relate to those programmes.

- 25 -

(50 on 4)

Tape # 6

    02.25.30 Take 1 (NG boom in)

    02.26.00   " 2 ✓

51	1	B	

SCENE 10

INT. DAY. OFFICE

CAMS 1B/C 2A/B   B1 A2

WS. SUE L FRAME
LESLEY R

SUE IS SITTING AT AN OFFICE DESK. LESLEY
IS PACING UP AND DOWN.

CRAB L. HOLD &
TIGHTEN TO MS LESLEY

LESLEY

Well I said to him - you can't have it

both ways Trevor - [~~you've got to get~~

~~your priorities straight~~] my lad` - either

52   2   A

MS SUE

we have a serious, meaningful relationship /

or I don't want to know.

02.26.35 Tk. 1 only

SUE

53   1   B

MS LESLEY

What did he say? /

LESLEY

                         a heavy commitment.

02.32.05   He said he didn't want ~~to get involved~~ (PAUSE)

54   2   A   Sue's reaction C|A   I mean, honestly! /

MS SUE

SUE

55   1   B

MS LESLEY

So what did you say? /

HOLD HER AS SHE SITS

LESLEY ~~(SITTING DOWN)~~

Well I said - how on earth do you know

at this stage of our relationship which

                         committed?

TIGHTEN TO MCU   of us is going to get ~~involved?~~ (PAUSE)(SHE SITS)

So he said he was sorry but he was just

plain scared of any ⌄serious (meaningful)

relationship.

(2 next)

Example of coverage script.

Fluidity of style

Light entertainment programmes, even when pre-recorded, often tend to be more fluid than drama, more like live programmes in that there are often last minute changes. Many shows work from a running order rather than a detailed script.

Involvement of artists

Because many light entertainment shows revolve around the personality of one or more artists, those artists will tend to be far more involved in the setting up of the production than on other types of programme. The host of a chat show will probably attend planning meetings and have a certain say in the guests chosen to appear on the show. A programme centred around a specific comedian will expect the artist to approve the script and dialogue and jokes may have to be altered to suit the comedian's personality.

Scripted shows

If there is a script it might well originate from a number of different writers. This can cause problems to the PA in the initial assembling of the material and she should bear in mind when it comes to the camera script that the document will be a rough guide only as there will doubtless be many changes made on the day of recording or transmission.

Estimating overall duration

It can be difficult trying to work out in advance the overall duration of the programme. Because pacing is the key to many comedians' routine, it is often not possible for the PA to work to the three words to a second rule which tends to hold good for presenters. Sometimes there might be pauses, for effect or for 'business' and comedians tend to speak at different speeds depending upon their style. Many of them ad lib during the recording or transmission and the PA will have to make allowances for all these factors when trying to work out timings. She will therefore have to work out whether to time hard on dialogue or adopt some more flexible system, bearing in mind that it will be difficult to be absolutely accurate on any assessment.

She will also have to allow for audience reaction time or time for 'canned' laughter where there is no studio audience and she must allow for applause.

In estimating the overall duration therefore, experience counts for a good deal. If the PA is familiar with the show, its style, its format and artists, she will be able to give a far more accurate assessment than one coming new to the programme.

Timings during recording or transmission

Because there are often studio audiences for light entertainment shows, even programmes that are recorded are usually done 'as live'. Because of this and because many light entertainment programmes are transmitted live, the PA must consider timing to be one of her priorities.

'She will also have to allow for audience reaction time or time for "canned" laughter . . .'

If the programme is recorded she should take timings at virtually every line as she can then work out with the director the precise timing for essential edits.

Timing music

Music plays a very large part in many light entertainment shows. The timing of music is very important for reasons of copyright and possible editing and durations should be noted at every verse or phrase of music.

Bar counting

Another element in many light entertainment programmes is that of counting through music items, known as bar counting. It must be remembered, however, that bar counting is not, of course, confined exclusively to light entertainment.

Bar counting is an extension of shot calling in that the PA counts the bars of music in order to keep everyone in the studio aware of the point reached in the musical item. It is especially important in music which is solely instrumental. A camera operator might have to make a move after the eighth bar and would be listening carefully to the PA's count.

Bar counting is a part of the PA's job which is sometimes viewed with alarm by otherwise experienced PAs who may have had little or no practice at the art and who might not be particularly musical.

How to accustom yourself to counting bars of music

If you find the whole concept strange and difficult to understand you might find it helpful to approach the job in various simple stages. The first stage is to become aware of the rhythmic beat in different pieces of music. Some music has a stronger and more obvious beat than others. Listen to various types of music and try tapping out the rhythm.

The next stage is to watch musical items on television and tap out the beat. Once you have the rhythm established you should try counting through the bars in each shot. With every shot change start again from one. This will begin to give you the feel of bar counting and will stand you in good stead when you come to do the real thing.

Music in your programme

If at all possible you should obtain a tape or disc of the music, take it home with you and play it over and over. Practice counting through the bars in the privacy of your own home and ensure that you can tap out the rhythm with confidence. The more familiar you are with the music, the better your bar counting will be in the studio.

If you cannot obtain the music in advance, don't panic.

Band calls

It is not likely that you would have to bar count 'cold' - that is without ever having heard the music played at least once. Most probably you would have a band call at which all the music would be played through. Good musicians will give you a bar breakdown at this stage. During the band call the director might work out his shots. He might then script them himself or call them out for you to note down. If the piece is instrumental you will need to count the bars between the shots as they are called out, in order to script them accurately.

Preparing a camera script

1. *Vocal.* You should type out the words of the song in the form of a standard camera script, noting any purely instrumental parts as necessary. If you know how many bars there are to each shot you should type those in, if not you should write them down as your first job in the gallery.
2. *Instrumental only.* It is helpful if you can read music and have the score in front of you. You could mark up the score with the shots. If you cannot read music or if there are no scores available you will have to rely on a form of script which might look something like this:

21. 2_____BASS (12 bars)

 L/A BASS PLAYER

 CRAB R & WIDEN

22. 1_____

 W/A. TRACK IN

 TO TIGHT 2-s   VIOLINS (24 bars)

23. 3 _____

   MS CONDUCTOR

                                    (8 bars)

24. 4 _____

   H/A W/A ORCHESTRA

                          ORCHESTRA (16 bars)

3. *'As directed'.* If the sequence is 'as directed' you will have to rely on the bar breakdown given during the band call and the knowledge you have gained during rehearsals. Time each shot in the 'as directed' sequence.

What do you say and how do you say it?

It is rather difficult to give a written down demonstration of bar counting. Given the example on page 151, however, you might say something like this:

   'Shot 51 . . . one of eight . . . two . . . three . . . four . . . five . . . six . . . seven . . . eight of eight . . .
   Shot 52 . . . one of eight . . . two . . . three . . . etc.
   Shot 53 . . . one of six . . . two . . .' and so on.

It is necessary to identify the shot by calling it 'Shot 2' rather than just '2' as one would when shot calling, in order to differentiate between the shots and the bars. Depending upon the music you might or might not have time to call out the number of the camera you are coming to next. If anything has to be omitted, that should. If the shots come thick and fast it might be more helpful to the studio if you just called the shot numbers while retaining the beat of the music by tapping it out.

On complex music items or productions there might be two PAs in the gallery, one to bar count and the other to call the shots.

Beating time

It helps to beat time when bar counting. Use a ruler, a pencil, anything, but do retain that firm, strong beat. If you become lost it will help you regain the rhythm.

Speak loudly

When bar counting it is especially important to speak clearly and loudly as your voice will be competing with the music.

Losing your place

If you lose your place or get it wrong when bar counting, my best advice is to keep quiet until you are sure you can restart correctly. That might be at the beginning of the next shot or on a fresh line of the song if you have numbered the bars against each line as in the example given below. Do not, whatever you do, try to catch up as you will only confuse everyone. Just keep the rhythm going by tapping it out, preview the shots and start when you feel confident.

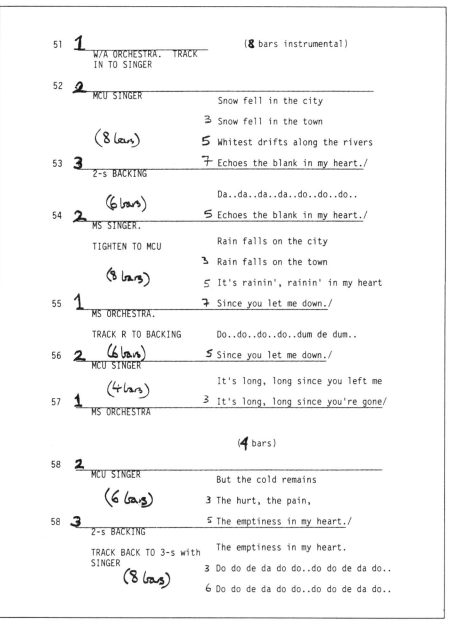

51 **1** (**8** bars instrumental)
W/A ORCHESTRA. TRACK
IN TO SINGER

52 **2**
MCU SINGER   Snow fell in the city

3 Snow fell in the town

(8 bars)   5 Whitest drifts along the rivers

53 **3**   7 Echoes the blank in my heart./
2-s BACKING

Da..da..da..da..do..do..do..

(6 bars)
54 **2**   5 Echoes the blank in my heart./
MS SINGER.

TIGHTEN TO MCU   Rain falls on the city

3 Rain falls on the town

(8 bars)   5 It's rainin', rainin' in my heart

55 **1**   7 Since you let me down./
MS ORCHESTRA.

TRACK R TO BACKING   Do..do..do..do..dum de dum..

56 **2** (6 bars)   5 Since you let me down./
MCU SINGER

(4 bars)   It's long, long since you left me

57 **1**   3 It's long, long since you're gone/
MS ORCHESTRA

(**4** bars)

58 **2**
MCU SINGER   But the cold remains

(6 bars)   3 The hurt, the pain,

58 **3**   5 The emptiness in my heart./
2-s BACKING

TRACK BACK TO 3-s with   The emptiness in my heart.
SINGER
(8 bars)   3 Do do de da do do..do do de da do..

6 Do do de da do do..do do de da do..

Example of typed out and marked up script of song.

9
Single camera shooting

The past few years have seen great strides in the development and use of lightweight, portable, electronic cameras and this fact, together with the advances made in the field of videotape editing, has meant that more and more programmes which used to be made on film are now being recorded on videotape.

The trend among directors is to utilize the greater freedom offered by these developments by shooting with a film-style technique: using a single camera and recording out of sequence. This method of shooting tends to combine the flexibility of the film-style with the economy of videotape.

What it means for the PA is that she must use her skills which are related to film when recording on to videotape. This can cause problems because of the split nature of her job.

The schizophrenic PA

In the past, the PA has been able to make a fairly clear distinction between:

(a) the electronic side of her work, i.e. sitting in a gallery or control room calling shots, timing, rolling, cueing, etc., and
(b) the film side of her work, i.e. standing by the camera shot listing and doing continuity.

In combining these two elements the PA is often left with a problem. Is her job to remain in the control room doing continuity from the monitor or should she be on the set, beside the camera? Can continuity be done adequately from a monitor? Some PAs tend to favour one method, some another. Both have advantages and disadvantages.

Advantages of remaining in the control room

1. You are with the director (providing he directs from the control room and not from the floor of the set).
2. You are at the centre of communications.
3. You can keep track of tape changes.
4. You can see the actual framing of the shot on the monitor.

5. You can spool back if there are any doubts over continuity.
6. You have time code displayed on the monitor.
7. You have a desk at which to spread your papers and are sheltered from inclement weather!

Disadvantages of remaining in the control room

1. You are not with the director (providing he directs from the floor of the set).
2. In such a situation you are no longer at the centre of communications. It is very difficult to explain points of continuity from the remoteness of the control room. Because of that you might feel distanced from the real centre of action, inhibited in making any continuity points and your authority in that area will pass to the floor manager, the stage manager and everyone else who is on the set. This will result not only in the important continuity aspect of your job being rendered ineffectual but in an enormous amount of time-wasting as everyone chimes in over points of continuity.
3. While you can see the actual framing of the shot on the monitor, you can only see it when the camera operator has finalized the shot. In order to do continuity properly you need to be watching and making notes during the entire setting up period.
4. It is very difficult to do continuity solely from the small, flat surface of the monitor. Having said that, however, I must in fairness add that there are PAs who have trained themselves to do just that.
5. While, unlike film, there is the advantage of being able to re-run material already recorded in order to check continuity, there is a very great danger that this could become the norm and an inordinate amount of time could be wasted during the shooting in checking back over tapes. Unless there is a genuine need, it is far better to rely on your notes for continuity.

Keeping a time code log while working on the set

If you feel that the continuity aspect of the job outweighs other considerations and that you would do the job far more effectively by being on the floor of the set beside the camera, you will need to work out some system whereby you can still compile a time-code log for editing. This could be resolved in a number of ways:

1. By arranging for 'real time' time code to be used. All you then need is a digital watch for the time on your watch would correspond to the time code on the tape.
2. If 'tape time' time code is preferred you could discuss with the engineers the possibility of having the time code displayed on a monitor on the set. This monitor could be used both for time code read-outs and for satisfying your need to know the framing of the shot.
3. If there is time between the shooting and the editing, you could have viewing copies made on cassette with time code inserted and compile a log after the shooting has been completed.

The director is the key

Your place during single camera shooting should ultimately be determined by the director. If the director tends to work from the floor then you should be beside him. If he works from the control room then that is your place. If he rehearses from the floor and watches the recording from the control room you will have a choice and should weigh up the need for continuity against other needs in making your decision.

'Your place during single camera shooting should ultimately be determined by the director.'

All I would say, finally, is that your decision should not be influenced by expediency. It is, after all, generally warmer and altogether more comfortable to remain in the control room – but will you be as competent at the job?

Preparing for location

Preparing for work on location follows much the same pattern whether you are filming, single camera shooting on videotape or planning a multi-camera outside broadcast. Important considerations such as scheduling, travel, food and accommodation are paramount.

The script

If there is a script it will have to be typed, either by yourself or the production secretary. There will be no camera script in single camera shooting but the director might require a shooting script to be typed out and distributed.

Meetings

There will be planning meetings of a technical nature, meetings with the costume and make-up supervisors and everyone connected with the production. Following these meetings you will be required to type out and distribute various forms, i.e. technical requirements, props, costume, make-up and so on, explained in more detail in earlier chapters.

Artists and extras

Artists and extras will have to be booked. You should remember that if a series is being shot, scenes from two or three different episodes might be recorded each day. This should be stated on the artists' contracts. In addition, you might have periods when you need to retain the artists, i.e. a few days, a week or even longer within the overall engagement period when the artist is not required on location. This must also be included in the contract.

Rehearsals

There might be a period of rehearsal before shooting, in which case you will have to book rehearsal rooms and send letters giving times and places to the artists.

Locations

The different venues for shooting will be found by the location manager or the floor manager. He or she will negotiate payment, get clearances with police and similar bodies, find adequate parking, power supplies and so on.

Travel

You will have to arrange adequate transport, book hire cars and generally ensure that you know precisely how everyone is getting to the location. If shooting is to take place overseas you should ensure that all travel arrangements are made in good time as air and shipping lines tend to get booked up. Check passports, visas, and ensure that correct vaccinations or inoculations are obtained if these are needed.

Accommodation

You will need to book suitable accommodation for the unit and that can be a difficult business as everyone will have different expectations and requirements. Do not forget that the more remote locations will probably have a scarcity of decent hotels and you should book as early as possible. Do not wait until you have the names of all the artists – block book rooms and send a detailed list later. Remember that it is better to overbook than be faced with irate artists or members of the production team who have no bed for the night. Would you be prepared to give them yours? And remember that you will never, ever satisfy every single person on the unit, no matter how hard you try.

Food

Neither will you satisfy everyone when it comes to making arrangements for eating. Faced with a gourmet's meal of smoked salmon, caviar and tempting home-made dishes there will be members of the unit who will slink off to the nearest cafe for fish and chips. If the unit is large enough it would be best for you to engage professional location caterers rather than rely on local restaurants. If the unit is small it might become your responsibility to find suitable eating places at each location.

Petty cash

On a small production you might be required to hold the petty cash, to pay for meals and accommodation and any incidental expenses incurred. This could lead to your having to carry vast sums of money around which would be a constant worry. Wherever possible you should arrange banking facilities in this country or overseas.

Schedule of recording

Sometimes the schedule of recording is worked out by the floor manager and sometimes by the PA in conjunction with the director. The schedule is organized with regard to the different locations, the amount of shooting at each location, the availability of artists and so on. Time should be allowed for travel from one location to the next and the regulations governing hours of work must be adhered to.

'Would you be prepared to give them yours?'

When the schedule has been finalized it should be typed out and distributed. As well as the details of the scenes to be recorded each day it should contain everything relevant to the shooting:

1. A cast list, together with agents' telephone numbers (artists' home numbers should be restricted to the immediate production team).
2. Detailed information on travel arrangements with maps to assist those driving to the locations.
3. A list of accommodation booked, the address and telephone number of the hotel, the dates and names of those booked in.
4. Details of the locations with addresses and telephone numbers of contacts.
5. Any other useful addresses or telephone numbers, i.e. local taxi service, doctor, police and so on.
6. Details of the technical equipment required, special props, etc.

Single camera shooting: continuity

Having mentioned the need for continuity when shooting single camera, film-style technique, just what is it?

What is continuity?

Continuity means being aware, both before and during the making of a programme of the final edited version, no matter in what order the material is recorded. It means trying to ensure, as far as possible, that when the programme is edited in its final form it will flow from shot to shot and scene to scene in a smooth manner with no continuity errors to distract the viewer.

Importance of continuity

The importance of continuity is greater than the popular misconception that it is only to do with hats and levels of drink in glasses. Continuity is not something that is solely confined to drama. A simple interview, a documentary, a magazine programme . . . whatever the content, so long as the technique of recording is by the use of one camera, shooting out of sequence, then continuity, to a greater or lesser extent, is required.

Doing the job

To go into the job of continuity in any great depth is outside the scope of this book and has been fully covered elsewhere.* But in this chapter I will try to set down the bare essentials of the job.

* Rowlands, A. (1977) *Script Continuity and the Production Secretary,* Focal Press.

Observation

The PA must watch the action of each shot and make relevant notes about what seems to be important in terms of matching shots. The information she builds up should be used during the recording to ensure that continuity of action, dialogue and props will be preserved from shot to shot and scene to scene.

What is important within a shot?

That, for anyone trying to do continuity on whatever type of programme, is the all-important question. First of all it must be realized that it is just not possible to watch *everything* within a shot. Neither is it necessary to do so. The art of continuity lies in the specialized and not generalized observation that is undertaken and there are a number of fairly simple guidelines that can be followed.

1. Framing

Without knowing the size of shot you cannot begin to do continuity. In a very wide shot, for example, it is not necessary to be as observant of all the actions as it would be in a close shot. It is generally true to say that the more that is happening in a shot, the less continuity matters. But, conversely, in a shot that does not have a lot of action, perhaps a close shot of two people, the smallest movement will be important. In shooting on videotape you have the advantage of being able to look at a monitor which will give the precise framing of each shot.

2. Largest moving object

Once the shot size is clear then the largest moving object within the shot is the most important to observe as a viewer's attention will be drawn to it – whether it is a head seen in close up, a person seen in mid shot or a large elephant entering frame and dominating the wide shot. Another general rule relates to colour. In the same way that the audience will tend to notice the largest moving object in the frame, they will also notice the brightest colours.

3. The main characters

If there is a great deal happening in the shot then you should concentrate on the main characters. Stick to watching the people the programme is about, the people who, theoretically, should hold the audience's interest and attention. Other people in the shot only assume importance *in relation* to the main subjects.

Given the above guidelines, what else does one need to notice?

Screen direction

Screen direction comes under the umbrella of continuity. Exits and entrances should always be noted and the information used to match shots preceding, following and cutting in to the master shot.

It is easy to become confused, especially if a number of different angles relating to the same scene are being shot. It helps to draw a quick, rough sketch of each shot, noting the camera position. When referring to exits and entrances always do so from the camera's point of view, which is also that of the audience. For example:

'The largest moving object within the shot is the most important to observe as a viewer's attention will be drawn to it . . .'

'Tom enters frame camera left and exits frame foreground right'. The convention is that if an object or person is to appear to be travelling in the same direction during a number of consecutive shots then they must always cross frame in the same direction.

A car is driving along the road. The camera is positioned so that the car appears to be travelling from left to right. Any subsequent shot intended to cut directly on to the first one must show that car travelling from left to right of frame. It is also permissible to show the car travelling straight to camera or directly away from camera. What will not work, however, is a shot of the car travelling from right to left. Cut directly on to the first shot, the car would appear to have changed direction.

Crossing the line

The principle of screen direction applies not just to movement. John and Jane are sitting opposite each other. John is on the left of frame, Jane on the right. These positions have been established in the master shot. Any other shot cutting directly on to or in to that master must feature John on the left and Jane on the right otherwise it would appear that the two people have changed places. The 'line' is an imaginary one drawn between people's noses as they look at each other. Providing the camera does not cross that line, shots that cut directly on to each other will match.

The only exceptions to this convention are as follows:

(a) When the camera moves during the course of a shot to a fresh position establishing Jane on the left of frame and John on the right.
(b) When the people move. Either John or Jane get up and move round to different positions.

Action in relation to dialogue

Another basic aspect of continuity is one which is often overlooked. It is, nevertheless, one of the most important points because it directly affects the editing process. Continuity of action, and especially action in relation to dialogue, is vital. Actions should be repeated at the same point on each shot and if dialogue is involved then it assumes even greater importance.

In working on scripted dialogue you should use the script as the basis of your notes and peg down the actions at the relevant places.

Costume notes

You should note the costumes worn by the actors in each shot and check that the same clothes are worn where there is direct continuity between shots and scenes.

Notes on props

Props can be divided into two distinct groups, dressing and action.

(a) Dressing props, i.e. furniture, etc., used to dress the set, do not, by and large, get moved (unless they are shifted in order to re-position camera and/or lights) and it is only necessary for you to have a general plot of these props.
(b) Action props are those used by the actors during the course of the action of a scene. It is therefore much more important that you know what these props are, where they are placed, when they are picked up or moved and at what point in relation to the dialogue.

Continuity is not in any sense a precise discipline. You might have noticed all the relevant things within a shot, your notes might be models of neatness and your drawings exquisite *but* there are other factors involved.

Artists

With the best will in the world – and most actors will try to do it right – some artists are not good on continuity and even the best will have 'off' days. Actors are people and not robots and that is something you should never forget.

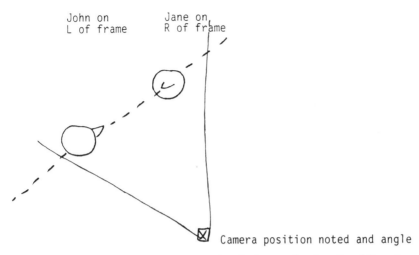

John on
L of frame

Jane on
R of frame

Camera position noted and angle

Dot in a line between people's noses as they look at each other. Providing the camera does not cross that line, shots that cut directly on to each other will match: i.e. John and Jane will remain on the same side of frame as in the original and will not 'jump' in frame.

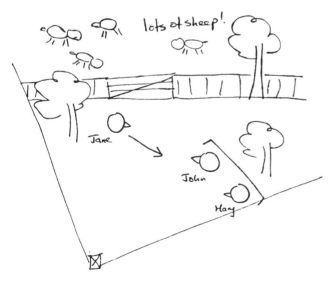

lots of sheep!

Jane

John

Mary

Always do a rough diagram of the shot, showing the camera position as well as the actors and main props. It does not matter how rough your diagram is, it will be of enormous help in matching future shots.

Directors

Directors too, are people, and even if you have noted wrong continuity it is by no means a foregone conclusion that the director will retake for that purpose. There are many reasons – many of them entirely valid – why a director will accept a shot which you feel to be wrong by virtue of continuity. There is nothing you can do about it.

Drawings

Always try to reduce the scene happening before your eyes to a simple sketch or drawing. It is far easier to relate to a sketch than to half a page of written description. The sketch need not be works of arts, indeed they are better if they are quick, rough and to the point, but they will be invaluable.

Keep close to the camera

Finally, in watching what is going on, keep as close to the camera as possible so that you are seeing the action from the same viewpoint. In addition, hold your script up on a level with the action in order to minimize the time between watching and writing. And if you can have a monitor somewhere within sight in order that you can check the framing then so much the better. Don't forget that while it is possible to spool back and re-run shots for continuity, it is an immensely time-wasting operation.

10

Post-production and the PA

Single camera shooting: information for the editor

Single camera shooting requires some form of record to be kept in order that the videotape editor and director have accurate information about what has been recorded when they come to reassemble the material in its correct order.

Unscripted programmes: shot lists

On an unscripted programme, for example a documentary, this shot list would be the only written information about the recording that exists, so it is extremely important that it is written both carefully and accurately.

The shot list would contain the following information:

1. Programme title, number, date of recording

2. Reel or cassette number

It is essential to write down the videotape reel or cassette number.

3. Location details

You should note down the location, whether interior or exterior, day or night. If exterior you should note the weather.

4. Visual identification of the shot

If there is time code, the 'in' point at the start of each shot should be noted down. If there is no time code then it would be useful to identify the shot in some way, possibly by using a film clapper board to show the shot and take. A verbal indent is also often given.

5. Shot description

An accurate description of the shot is the next essential. A list of the most commonly used shot descriptions and their explanations is given in Chapter 7. A basic shot description would suffice for a scripted programme but if unscripted a fuller description would be helpful, i.e. who was in shot, how they entered frame, how they exited and so on.

6. *Interviews*

When compiling a shot list of an interview it is important to note down the questions asked by the interviewer and give an outline of the reply.

7. *Takes*

Some of the most important details to note relate to the number of takes for each shot. If the action of the shot is unsatisfactory for one reason or another, it is repeated again and again until the director is satisfied. A note should always be made of the number of takes relating to each particular shot, the good takes marked and the reason given why the others were considered unsatisfactory (NG).

8. *Timing*

You should take a stopwatch timing of each take of each shot. Time the action only, from when the director says 'cue' to when he says 'cut' or 'stop recording'. This timing will be useful in editing and also for building up a cumulative running time of the programme.

Scripted programmes

On scripted programmes, drama for example, you would provide basically the same information presented in a different way as you have the advantage of being able to provide the editor with a script.

1. *Record of shooting*

This record, which is similar to an abbreviated shot list, could be typed out as one long list or it could be presented in the film fashion of putting each shot on a separate sheet of paper or small index card.

2. *Coverage script*

You should provide the editor with a marked up coverage script, each line denoting a shot and the shot identified by means of the 'in' point of time code and the video-tape reel or cassette number.

All this information is primarily for use *after* recording has been completed. Any notes, drawings or photographs taken *during* the recording which relate to the day-to-day continuity of matching one shot with another while recording is in progress are of no interest to the editor.

Videotape editing

In the 1950s, videotape was edited by cutting and splicing the master recorded tape. These edits were very 'hit and miss' as there was no way of previewing an edit

SHOT LIST

"STATELY HOMES"   Dir: Peter McDonnell   21st February 1986

Programme number: 21Z/367942/B   VTR No: 31548

Location: Withyton House, Staffs

T/C 'IN'	TAKE	SHOT DESCRIPTION	DUR.	OK/NG
10.05.00	1	EXTERIOR: HOUSE & GROUNDS Wide establishing shot of house from gates - looking down tree lined drive	.45	OK
10.12.05	1	Z/O from house to WS a/b	1.00	NG - person in shot
10.16.20	2	a/b	1.05	OK
10.32.45	1	Start wide and z/i to house	.20	NG - cam
10.43.40	2	a/b	.55	OK
		EXTERIOR : SUNKEN GARDEN		
11.55.10	1	WS panning L-R to gazebo	.40	NG - cam wobble
11.57.28	2	a/b	.42	OK
12.14.48	1	WS panning R-L (starting on gazebo)	.47	OK
		INTERIOR : DRAWING ROOM Interview with Lord and Lady Corley		
14.35.20	1	2-s Lord and Lady Corley on sofa Q: Lord and Lady Corley, this beautiful house is an amalga-mation of many different styles of architecture. When was the first building constructed? A: (Lord C) There has been a house on this site since Elizabethan times...west wing.. fire...restoration in Jacobean times..bits added by each succeeding generation. Q: And have you added anything? A: (Lady C) The vegetable garden and sunken garden altered	6.40	OK

Example of a shot list.

decision before cutting up the tape. Sound editing was a further problem as the sound was about 9″ in front of the picture. The videotape that was used in broadcasting organizations was two inches wide and known as the Quadruplex system.

The development of electronic editing in the early 1960s meant that the master tape was no longer physically chopped up. Instead the material was re-recorded on to a second tape, reassembled into its final programme order. This system is known as 'dub' editing and is the basis of all videotape editing done today. Early electronic editing was a fairly haphazard system, despite the introduction of Editek in 1963 which controlled the edit point electronically.

When time code was introduced in 1967 enabling a more precise control of the edit point than ever before, videotape editing became more efficient and accurate.

The establishment of one inch videotape with a helical scan arrangement in 1978 meant that it became possible to stop the tape and replay the same track repeatedly, thus providing a 'frozen' picture. It also became possible to offer slow motion replay.

The later developments of computer controlled systems has meant that the director and editor can enjoy the more sophisticated, precise editing that used to be the sole province of film. But dub editing does have an inherent problem.

Problem of dub editing

The basic difficulty of the system of re-recording material from one reel to another is that every time the material is transferred there is a loss of picture quality. Each successive re-recording is known as a different 'generation', the first generation being the master recorded tape, the second generation being the first re-recording of the material and so on. In broadcast television it is considered inadvisable to transmit more than the third generation.

So why is this a problem? In order to examine that, we have to look at the basic way film is edited.

Film editing

In film editing using the negative/positive film stock, the shot material is processed and is in a negative form. From this negative a print, the 'rush' print, is made together with the sound track which has been recorded separately but synchronously with the picture. Picture and sound are physically broken down, cut up into individual shots.

The editing is done by joining these shots together in whatever order is decided upon by the director and editor. Shots can be experimented with in any order, they can be lengthened, shortened, replaced or re-cut at any point. It does not matter what state the print gets into: the print is only a guide for the negative cutter who splices the negative *only* after all the creative decisions have been finalized. This allows immense flexibility. It means that changes can be made at any time until the negative is cut. Once the negative is cut the transmission print or prints can be made without loss of picture quality since they are made directly from the picture negative.

Another consideration of film editing is that the equipment used in the cutting room is relatively inexpensive as it does not have to produce images of transmission quality.

Videotape editing

With dub editing on videotape, the restriction upon the number of generations one can go to without severe loss of picture quality means that ideally the editor should get it right the first time, not necessarily in terms of shots, but in terms of overall length of the programme.

It would be possible to leave a gap of, say 20″ in the middle of an edited pro-gramme knowing that you have a shot of exactly 20″ to drop in, but if you want to drop in a shot of only 15″ then either all the edits from that point to the end of the programme will have to be re-made – a tedious and time-consuming operation – or you will have to go to another generation of tape, i.e. copy all the shots up to the 15″ shot, edit in that shot and then copy the edited end section.

'These edits were very "hit and miss".'

Apart from all this, in spending a long time deliberating and trying out various artistic and creative options in videotape editing means tying up a vast amount of highly expensive machinery – expensive because it must reproduce pictures of transmission quality at every stage.

So, how to get round the difficulties?

Off-line editing

Off-line editing means that the 'rushes', i.e. the original material, whether it has been recorded on one inch videotape or some other form, is copied generally on to some inferior form of tape which uses less expensive equipment for recording and playback, i.e. VHS, Low Band U-Matic, Betamax (see Chapter 13 for explanation of these forms). The time code which has been recorded on to the master tape would be 'burned in' to this copy. The director can then off-line edit in the following ways:

1. He can take the copy home, sit comfortably in front of his television – preferably with a glass of his favourite beverage to hand – watch the recorded material and make notes, using the time code as a point of reference, on the way he wishes the master material to be assembled.
2. He can do the same job but less comfortably in the office, using his PA to make the notes.
3. He can gain access – which the PA might be required to book – to an edit suite, with or without an editor, and do an assembly by dub editing the material in the required order on to another VHS, Low Band U-Matic or whatever. This process can be gone through any number of times, enabling the director to experiment, change his mind, lengthen or shorten shots, etc. He can go to as many generations as he likes providing he can get some sort of image on the monitor. The quality of picture is irrelevant as this copy will not be transmitted.

The other advantage to this off-line system of editing is that the director is not tying up expensive equipment while this essential creative process takes place.

When all the decisions have been made, the director can then go into the 'on-line' editing session and the master tape will be edited. There will then be only one generation between the original and the transmitted tape.

The PA's job in off-line editing would be to make an assembly order for the videotape editor. She should note down the tape reel numbers (of the *master* tapes, the reel numbers of the viewing copies are irrelevant) and the 'in' and 'out' point of time code of the edited copy. It is especially important in off-line editing that the reel numbers of the master material are identified on the off-line editing cassettes.

On-line editing

The PA usually attends the on-line editing sessions. She goes to them armed with the log she has made and gives the editor the information he needs: which master tape reels to use in order and the time code information.

Many programmes do not need any off-line editing and sometimes it is not feasible or possible for off-line editing to take place. In that case the PA and director will be faced with editing the master tape direct from the recording with no stage in between.

The PA would take to this editing her notes from the recording and, if a scripted programme, her coverage script marked up as explained earlier.

Video conforming

If all editing decisions have been completely finalized in an off-line editing situation and no creative decisions are to be made at the on-line editing stage, then the on-line editing is often known as video conforming, since each shot is edited solely by reference to its time code and not to its picture content.

Film conforming

When total flexibility of the film editing and dubbing is required, especially in a mixed media programme where the original material might exist on anything from two inch videotape to amateur-shot Super 8mm film or even amateur video, a system known as film conforming can be used.

'He can take the copy home, sit comfortably in front of his television – preferably with a glass of his favourite beverage to hand – watch the recorded material and make notes.'

Anything which does not originate on one inch videotape is transferred to one inch. In the case of specially shot film it will often be advantageous to electronically convert the original negative picture to a positive form (phase reverse). The pictures from the one inch videotapes are then transferred on to a 16mm colour reversal film recording. The sound is recorded on to conventional 16mm magnetic film in synchronization with the picture. Editing and sound dubbing then proceed exactly as the normal film editing process up to the point where there is a 16mm finalized cutting copy and a final mix sound track. This sound track is transferred to one inch videotape and the picture material conformed to match the cutting copy by means of a computerized system involving time code information on the film recording. Any grading or colour matching or digital video effects are incorporated at this stage. The grading is done electronically rather than photographically as with film.

Booking videotape editing facilities

If you are responsible for booking editing facilities then you should, wherever possible, discuss with the videotape editor precisely what is needed before you fill in any forms. If, for example, a mix is needed then three machines would have to be booked. If you require something like a wipe or any special effects you would need to book a digital video effects generator. It is not necessary that you should have the technical expertise to know exactly what is required for your programme – it is sufficient for you to know that there are many areas in television which are both complex and intensely specialized and for which you need expert help.

Sound

Sound is so often the poor relation to picture in television. It is wrong to think of it in this way; sound can bring pictures alive by the use of music, and different effects can add immeasurably to the overall creative effect.

Sound is recorded simultaneously on to videotape along with the picture. On one inch videotape anything up to four audio tracks are available, but one is normally used for recording time code. Therefore in videotape editing a simple sound mix can be done at the same time as the picture is edited. If the sound post production is complex a separate dub may take place after the editing.

What is a dub?

A certain amount of confusion arises over the use of the term 'dub' which can have three separate meanings:

(a) Making a copy of an existing audio or video recording.
(b) Re-voicing dialogue, e.g. 'I saw a French film last night which had been dubbed into English'.
(c) Dubbing, dubbing session or post production dub are all names given to the process of mixing together the various sound tracks – location sound, commentary, music, library sound effects and any post-synchronized material – to form a master sound track for the programme. In broadcast television this operation

normally takes place in a dubbing theatre although some post production houses incorporate a multi-track sound recorder in their editing suites to allow the dubbing to take place there.

If there is to be a sound dub at a later stage in videotape post production, the actuality sound will be laid off from the master videotapes on to one or more audio tracks of the edited videotape. Before the dub can take place, a non-transmission copy of the picture is made, normally on Low Band U-Matic (see Chapter 13) which has two audio tracks. One of these is generally used for a guide soundtrack and the other is used to record the time code from the edited videotape. At the same time the sound from the edited videotape is lifted off on to one or more tracks of a multi-track tape recorder. One of the tracks on this tape recorder is used to record the time code from the master edited videotape. This multi-track tape recorder is equipped with an electronic synchronizer which enables it to slave itself to a time code signal, thus it will run exactly in sync with time code played from the U-Matic or the edited transmission videotape.

In the dubbing theatre additional sound will be laid on to other tracks of the multi-track recorder, using the picture from the Low Band U-Matic as a guide. When all the sound likely to be required has been assembled in this way, the various audio tracks are mixed together to form the final sound track which is recorded on one of the spare tracks of the multi-track recorder, again using the Low Band U-Matic as a guide. Time code is displayed from the recording on the Low Band U-Matic.

When everyone is satisfied with the final mixed soundtrack, the multi-track recording is taken back to the videotape editor who lays it back on to the master edited videotape.

If there is to be any sound post production, therefore, it is imperative that the master edited videotape has time code on it.

What does a PA do?

The PA might be required to find library effects, tapes or discs for the dub. During the final run through of the master sound track the PA should time any music for copyright purposes.

Specially composed music/commentary

If music is to be composed specially for the programme, or if there is narration or commentary to be written, a copy of the master edited tape will have to be organized, preferably on to Low Band U-Matic or VHS and sent to the composer/writer. This copy should have time code burned in. When the time comes to record the music or commentary, if this is to be done in a separate sound session from the dub, it is important to arrange for a copy of the master edited videotape, again normally Low Band U-Matic to be available. This copy should not only have the time code *displayed* in the picture area for the convenience of cueing, but also have an actual *recording* of the time code on one of its audio tracks so that music or commentary can be recoded on to a tape which is synchronized with the picture as in the dubbing process.

Commentary script

If the PA is required to type a script for the commentary it should be typed in treble spacing, with the time code 'in' points (of the edited tape time) on the left hand side. A wide margin should be left for notes and alterations. Sentences should never be carried forward from one page to another. When typing the time code, it is often more convenient for the hours and frames to be left off.

TIMECODE	COMMENTARY
00.02	The sad story of the East and West Junction and South Wales Mineral Railway is an object lesson in how the entrepreneurial spirit of the Victorians did not always flourish.
01.59	Conceived in 1874 by a flamboyant Welshman, Alun Thomas, its ambitious scheme was to link the blast furnaces in South Wales with iron ore from Northamptonshire mines after local stocks were used up.
02.45	Sadly, the expected traffic never materialised and by 1901 the Company was in a sorry state.

Example of a commentary script.

Clearing up

Representative sample of forms

Programme as completed (transmitted/televised/recorded)
Final estimate of external costs
Release of artists' fees/artists' payments call sheet
Transmission form/Programme timing report/Videotape timing and continuity
Post production script
Billings
'Thank you' letters

Once the programme has been recorded and the editing and dubbing taken place, it is by no means the end of the production for the PA. There now follows a positive deluge of forms to be filled in and circulated before the PA can throw the left-over scripts into the wastepaper basket (after ensuring that some are retained for posterity) and banish the programme file to whatever vault, basement or building houses dead files.

Even on live programmes the PA has a certain amount of clearing up, although that is usually minimal compared to the clearing up necessary on recorded programmes. What, however, is basic to all television programmes, whether live or recorded is a form itemizing in detail the entire content of the programme. This form is vital both as a written record for possible future use of the programme (a second transmission, overseas sales, made into cassette form for home sales, etc.), for any enquiries relating to any part of the programme and for all details of copyright.

This form goes under different names, but the essential information contained therein would be the same.

Programme as completed (transmitted/televised/recorded)

1. General details

The name of the programme, the production or job number, the VTR number and reel numbers of other tapes must be given. The date of recording and/or transmission should be shown. Information on the studio or OB site used for the recording, the names of the producer, director and PA also come under the general details.

2. Content and contributors

A synopsis of the programme should be written and everyone appearing in it must be noted. If scripted, the name of the author (and adapter), address and telephone number and details of the writer's agent. The names of all the contibutors, whether artists, presenters, extras or members of the public must be listed. The kind of contract the contributors were employed under, details of their days of rehearsal and performance days in the studio or on location. The names of all musicians, the contract issued to them, the instruments they play, the dates of rehearsal and recording and the type of session for which they were booked. The type of music (theme, incidental, etc.) that was being recorded must be given. If any facilities were used, i.e. a stately home, location caterers, a preserved steam railway, these must be included on the form.

3. Copyright details

Any book or publication used in the programme must be noted, together with the name of the author, the date of publication, the publisher and whether or not the book is in copyright. The same information is required for book illustrations. Any still photographs used must be written down: whether they are black and white or colour; their reference number and description and details of the copyright holder.

4. Film/videotape inserts

(a) *Film.* The title of the film used and its source, i.e. whether it was specially shot for the programme or came from elsewhere, possibly stock shots from the company's film library or bought in. The original source of the material *must* be stated. It is not enough to use a piece of film from another production and then state the source to be the name of that production. Where did that earlier production gain the film from – in other words who owns the copyright? It is essential to trace film back to its original source in order to ensure that payment is made to the correct person. In addition, the gauge of film used, i.e. 16mm, 35mm, the running time and whether sound or silent must be noted.
(b) *Videotape.* The same information is required for videotape inserts as for film, i.e. the tape reel numbers, the format (2″, 1″ and so on), the source of the material for copyright reasons and the running time.

If the videotape insert is of old film that has previously been recorded on tape you must note that there is a film content in your programme and trace the film back to its original source.

5. Music

For copyright information the following details need to be noted: the composer, publisher and arranger of the music; the performer, the title of the piece and, if on a record, which side and which band. The duration of the music used in the programme must be noted and a full description of its use: was it specially composed for the programme, is it background music, is it incidental music, visual or non-visual?

Other clearing-up work the PA might have to do could include:

Final estimate of external costs

Some companies require a costing of certain external items to be compiled by the PA. The items to be costed would vary from company to company and you should follow the system in use and take advice before completing this form.

Release of artists' fees (artists' payments call sheet)

A note might need to be sent to the contracts department stating that work has been satisfactorily completed in order that the final payments can be made.

Details of the days and hours of work of each artist must be made and sent to the relevant department for overtime and supplementary payments.

In the case of children being employed, the most careful notes have to be kept by the PA of the hours of work, of rest and of tuition for each child and these details must be submitted to the authority concerned.

PROGRAMME AS TELEVISED

SERIES TITLE & NO. IN SERIES		PROGRAMME TITLE		PROD NO	VTR NO
DATE OF VTR	DATE OF TXM	STUDIO OR OB SITE		TAPE NOs	
PRODUCER	ELIGIBLE/NOT ELIGIBLE FOR RESIDUALS (Delete as applicable)	DIRECTOR		ELIGIBLE/NOT ELIGIBLE FOR RESIDUALS (Delete as applicable)	
PRODUCTION ASSISTANT		PA's SIGNATURE		EXT	DATE
FILM TITLE (AND SOURCE)			GAUGE	RUNNING TIME	
				SOUND	SILENT	STOCK OR SPECIALLY SHC

PROGRAMME AS TELEVISED   2
(Continuation sheet)

PROGRAMME TITLE		PROD. NO.	PLACE OF REHEARSAL
RUNNING TIME	PRODUCTION ASSISTANT & EXT. NO.		
NAME OF ARTISTE	REHEARSAL DATES	PERFORMANCE DAY(s)	COMMENTS

PROGRAMME AS TELEVISED 3 — MUSICIANS

| PROG. TITLE | | PROD. No. | VTR No. |

Names and Addresses* of Musicians and Instruments played	Date	No. in Group or band	Rehearsal prior to Basic Session		BASIC SESSION							COMMENTS Incl. Session type** travel, subsistence, title of music when applicable.
			From	To	REHEARSAL		VTR/TX/SOUND RECORDING		OVERTIME			
					From	To	From	To	From	To		

PROGRAMMES AS TELEVISED

PROGRAMME TITLE		PRODUCTION NO.	VTR NO.
MUSIC			
PERFORMER	TITLE OF MUSICAL WORK	COMPOSER	PUBLISHER	RECORD NO. & LABEL	DESCRIPTION OF USE State whether visual or background/vocal or instrumental	DURATION

Example of programme as televised form.

Transmission form (Programme timing report/Videotape timing and continuity)

These forms – given different names by different companies – all relate to the transmission of the programme and are essentially for presentation. Firstly the programme needs to be identified clearly by its name, production number and videotape number. The recording and transmission dates are required. Details of the opening shots (both sound and vision) and the closing shots should be shown. The programme's overall duration must be stated, the duration of the end sequence and part timings for commercial breaks. Any other information that would be helpful to the transmitting of the programme should be given on this form, i.e. a moving or dramatic end, a sustained period of silence, the absence of pictures, a presentation announcement to be made and so on. Sometimes a synopsis and cast list is required.

Post production script

A post production script is usually required for archive purposes. This should be a marked up, totally accurate script, if the programme was scripted. It should be accurate in that it should be *post*-editing and not *pre*-editing. Cuts might have taken place in the editing for example and these should be reflected in the script.

If the programme was unscripted a script must be made with a time code column, a column for pictures and a column for sound.

Billings

This is the information for the published programme guide. It should contain general details about the programme: the title, the author, the adapter, the episode number and title, the transmission day, date and time and the VTR number. The type of programme, a contact for any queries, the cast list, production credits, a brief synopsis and points of special interest also need to be given.

Publicity

Publicity material for the programme might need to be organized by the PA and press showings arranged.

Co-productions

If the programme is a co-production then a great deal of extra work is generated. At every stage of the programme the PA should be aware of the involvement of others, for example, in the clauses to be included in artists' contracts. Copies of the final programme might need to be made for the co-producer(s), music and effects tracks made and a good deal of liaison would take place, probably on a PA to PA level.

Overseas sales of the programme, cable and satellite sales, cassettes for home sale, all these will require a certain amount of additional work by the PA.

'Thank you' letters

Don't forget to send 'thank you' letters to everyone who has helped in the making of the programme, especially those outside television. They are always appreciated.

And finally . . .

Throw away a mountain of unwanted paper, send the programme file to its final resting place, clear out your desk, unpin the wall charts, take home the potted plants and everything else that made the office home for the last few months . . . and prepare to start again on Monday morning with a fresh director, a fresh programme . . .

And remember that the ghost of this production will haunt you for many months to come . . .

'Send the programme file to its final resting place.'

Part Three
The wider world of television: the itinerant PA

11
The freelance PA

The more fluid direction that television has taken over the years has given rise to the freelance PA - that infinitely adaptable creature who will travel at a moment's notice to Potters Bar or Peking and will arrive, cool, capable and with stopwatch to the fore, ready to exercise any one of her many specialized skills.

Where do freelance PAs come from?

Freelance PAs are made, not born, although sometimes they can slide into the system from unknown sources. They tend to come from three distinct areas:

(a) The major television companies. Trained PAs who have enjoyed all the privileges and comforts of a pensionable job will, for a variety of reasons, throw it all up in favour of the life on the road, the nomadic existence of the freelance. Because these PAs have been trained by one of the major companies they generally have more to offer in the way of skills, although it must be remembered that their experience might have been limited within the company for whom they worked.

(b) The production companies. The PA who has worked up from clerk or secretary to become PA and who decides to go freelance can face some major problems. Depending upon the output of the production company their experience might have been limited to one aspect of the PA's job only. They could find difficulties in the freelance market where a range of skills is expected.

(c) The unknown. Some freelance PAs find themselves in that position almost by default. They might have been employed in some capacity by a very small company. When the production is finished they are footloose, fancy free and in need of earning a living. What better way than by becoming a freelance PA?

Training of PAs

At the time of writing there is a distinct need for some form of standardized training of PAs in the freelance sector of television. The job of a PA is far more than being solely a super secretary. There are specific skills to be learnt which can only be fully assimilated in a practical way through experience.

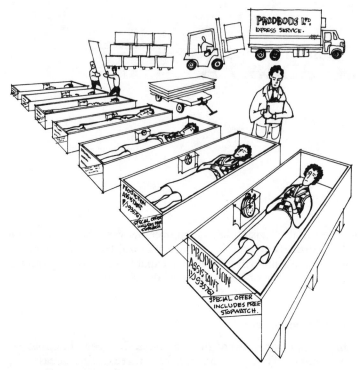

'There is a distinct need for some form of standardized training of PAs in the freel-ance sector of television.'

The freelance PA's job

The work involved for a freelance PA is, by and large, similar to the work a PA might be required to do in any area of television, the programmes themselves determining the particular skills called for.

Freelance PAs will, generally speaking, be less involved in the setting up of a production but will have greater involvement during the period of their engagement. In some cases the PA would be employed strictly for their specialized skills, whether in the gallery or on location. The PA might be called back for the editing depending on the complexity of the post production work.

Who employs the freelance PA?

The large television companies might employ freelance PAs in order to fill a gap, cover for holiday periods and so on. The large companies generally keep a list of PAs who have worked for the company before and therefore know the system.

Production companies large and small will employ freelance PAs. Cable and satellite TV stations might also employ freelance staff. Sometimes facility houses will employ a freelance PA for a specific job.

Production companies making programmes for television

Recent years have seen enormous changes taking place in broadcast television in the UK. With the introduction of Channel 4, cable and satellite, has come the breaking up to a certain extent of the monopoly of the main television companies.

A bewildering number of production companies and facility houses, often with exotic names, have sprung up and it might be as well to try to group them as far as possible before looking at the work of the PA in the freelance sector.

1. Facility houses

The facility houses do not originate programmes, they merely hire out specialized facilities, i.e. studios, editing, camera equipment, etc., to individual groups, consortiums, or anybody wishing to make a programme. The facility house will tend to specialize in just one technical area of the making of a programme. Facility houses do have their own staff: a group of videotape editors and engineers might form their own facility house offering a range of post production facilities, camera and sound operators might do likewise, but PAs are not usually in-built in this system. If a PA is required a freelance would be engaged.

2. Small production companies

A production company can be as small as one person – often a producer or director – with an idea for a programme. He or she might form a company, acquire a desk and telephone, perhaps engage a secretary and get on with it. It can obviously be a great deal larger than that, but the small company would undoubtedly have to go to a facility house in order to employ the expertise needed in making the programme. A freelance PA would be employed for the duration.

3. Large production companies

Some of these companies also operate as facility houses for others as well as making their own programmes.

Some of the companies employ permanent staff, including PAs: many of them operate solely with freelance staff, production people being taken on as and when required.

4. Companies that specialize

Some of the larger production companies tend to specialize in making one type of programme and all their resources go into the specific requirements needed to satisfy that format. This is following the trend in the USA where whole channels are devoted to one specific type of production. This means, of course, that the PA's work in that company will be wholly geared to the programme's needs. The difficulty for the individual PA arises when they feel limited within the company for whom they work but are unable to move elsewhere as they have never learnt the other skills needed by a PA.

'A production company can be as small as one person.'

Cable and satellite broadcasting

The PA underground

Cable television is widespread in the USA but still relatively new in the UK. Cable is the means by which individual homes can receive television - literally through cables laid underground. Once the cable is laid, homes can receive any one of a number of channels, including the existing major television channels. The number that can be received varies: in the USA the cable viewer has access to a vast number; in the UK the choice is at present more limited.

The cable television station is an operator who is licensed to provide:

(a) a variety of channels each showing ready made programmes which have originated from a number of different sources: television companies throughout the world, films, production companies and so on;
(b) their own channels showing programmes they have made themselves, either live or pre-recorded.

The viewer is therefore provided with a number of different television channels, some of them offering a range of programmes, many tending to specialize in one type: a news channel, a sports channel, a children's channel, a music channel, a channel showing films and so on.

The job of the cable television PA

The PA might be a full-time employee of the cable television company or might be freelance. She will not be involved in the transmission of programmes. That is done by transmission controllers who work out the schedules, make sure the tapes are in transmission control, work out the advertising slots and roll the tapes in the scheduled order.

The PA, however, might be responsible for the tape library.

Because the companies tend to be smaller than those of the major channels, the PA might find herself doing a lot of the work which would be delegated to others in larger companies. In the studio, for example, she might operate the caption generator and for location she might carry a good deal of the responsibility for setting up, finding locations, scheduling and so on. Or again, a researcher might be employed on a freelance basis for this work and the PA's job would become far more desk-bound and secretarial.

The cable companies' own programmes tend to fall into the following categories:

1. live news/magazine type programmes
2. documentary style programmes of local interest
3. community access programmes.

The PA would therefore need the skills required for working on this range of productions – a lot of gallery work including timing, rolling and cueing as well as the ability to compile shot lists and log time codes.

'... the PA might find herself doing a lot of the work which would be delegated to others in larger companies.'

The PA in space

Broadcasting by no means of satellite is by means new. Many world events are beamed directly to the main television stations by satellite. What is relatively new in the UK and Europe however is the private commercial television station operating throughout several countries by means of satellite.

Where do programmes come from?

Some satellite stations originate their own material. Some operate with a mix: their own programmes, ones from television companies throughout the world, from smaller production companies, films, international news agencies and so on.

How do they operate?

They operate by using a communications satellite which can be used to broadcast to, say, the whole of Europe. Signals are transmitted up to the satellite then re-transmitted back to earth at a different frequency where they are picked up on satellite receiving dishes by licensed cable companies. The signals are scrambled in code and each licensed operator has a decoder at his cable headend to de-scramble signals before they are distributed to the subscriber's home via cable. This provides a check for copyright purposes.

Transmission

Transmission Controllers (TC) and Assistant Transmission Controllers (ATC) run the operation of co-ordinating and transmitting programmes. The TC's have overall responsibility but Production Assistants have acted as ATCs and it is a natural progression.

Originating programmes

The PAs job both in satellite and cable companies is very similar to the work of any PA on the production of a programme except that she will tend to concentrate on the technical aspects of the job.

The Programme Organizer will be responsible for much of the setting up, the booking of facilities and artists and so on.

Standardized format

Whatever the original format of the programme – film, VTR in all its manifestations and programmes from different television systems – they would all be converted to the system operating in the receiving country (PAL system in the UK and Europe, excluding France) and the material would be transferred to 1″ videotape. The PA, however, is not involved in organizing these transfers.

The PA in space.

Pop promotions and commercials

The PA working for a production company making pop promotions ('promos') of records or commercials for advertising agencies will find her work very varied. She will tend to work directly to the producer and be the central administrator in the production. Her role is primarily an organizational one and she might find that she is not required to have the more specialized technical skills of either studio gallery work or continuity, although she will need a good grasp of the technical requirements that go to make up the production.

Setting up

In working both on commercials and pop promotions the PA often has a lot of responsibility. She will be responsible for booking all the facilities, with the exception of costume and props which are dealt with by specialists engaged for that purpose.

She will have to book the film or video crews, their equipment, lighting, location transport, meals, accommodation and so on, working within the budget laid down by the producer. She will need to get permission to shoot at different locations and liaise with the police and members of the public. She will obtain copyright clearances if necessary.

On a pop promotion the PA will book any artists and extras required and negotiate their fees, whereas on a commercial, although the PA will set up auditions, the advertising agency and their clients will confirm the artists and deal with their fees.

The PA will do any typing required, including typing the script. She will issue call sheets for the shoot.

The shoot

Commercials and pop promos. always used to be made on 35mm film and many still are, but there is an increasing trend towards recording on to videotape.

The PA might be required to shot list or provide a log for editing and she might be asked to do simple continuity. Usually, however, the director will compile his own shot list and if continuity is involved a script supervisor will be employed.

During the shoot the PA will have enough to do with sorting out any hitches, making phone calls and doing whatever else is necessary to ensure a smooth recording. On a large shoot she will have a number of 'runners' working directly under her.

Post production

The PA will book all editing whether film or videotape. She will organize and book transfers – from film to one inch videotape, from one inch to U-Matic or whatever. If the post production work includes specialized computer effects machines, the PA will book the necessary facilities. She will organize the sound dubs.

Her other post production work will consist of writing 'thank you' letters and making final payments.

Generally the advertising agency or record company will receive a one inch dub off the master videotape (the master being held by the production company). The advertising agency or record company will organize their own distribution and the PA will not be responsible for the making of additional copies.

Pop promos

These can vary in time and complexity from a half a day's simple shoot to something extending over a number of days with a great deal involved in terms of resources and sophistication.

Pop promos are made for record companies who, by and large, tend to leave the production company alone after approving the intitial script. They will allow the director to use his own creative skills in fashioning the promo. and will not be breathing down his neck at every stage of production.

Commercials

The opposite is true of commercials where there is far more direct involvement on the part of the advertising agency and its client during every stage of production.

The agency itself will produce a storyboard – which shows in pictures every single shot to be taken – and there will be a whole number of pre-production meetings before the shoot. The reason for this is not hard to find and very understandable. A great deal of money is involved in the screening of commercials and every single second of the commercial is therefore important. The budget tends to be high and the shooting ratio, which is the ratio of film or tape shot to that used in the final production, is equally high – often around 60:1 as against around 10:1 for the average television drama.

The PA's job in all this is therefore a key one of public relations. She will maintain close liaison with the advertising agency and keep them informed on everything that happens concerning their production.

'During the shoot the PA will have enough to do with sorting out any hitches, making phone calls and doing whatever else is necessary to ensure a smooth recording.'

Part Four

Getting away from television: the non-broadcast PA

12

Non-broadcast use of videotape

Over the past few years video has expanded in all kinds of areas outside television. One has only to look at the video recorder in the home and the growing market for lightweight video cameras to record weddings, parties, holidays and baby on the lawn to see just how video has become integrated into people's lives – people to whom the processes that go into the making of a television programme would have been shrouded in mystery and mystique only a short time ago.

To meet this expanding market, cameras and equipment have become lighter, easier to handle and simpler to use.

We live in the age of instant pictures. Pictures are easier to assimilate than the written word and two generations have now been brought up with television as an indispensable item of furniture – an entertainer, a teacher, a friend. An explanation therefore of a new security system, of company policy, of different training methods, or simply how to work the new cooker that has arrived in the staff canteen is clearly better done by exploiting the potential of video. This thinking is not new. Some large industrial companies have had their own film units for years but the revolution in video technology has meant its expansion in the field of industrial training.

In other fields, too, the growth of video over the last decade has been astounding. In education, in schools and colleges, video has been used not just to make learning more pleasant and more relevant but the making of the programmes themselves has become an educational study.

In health, research and education, video has been found to be of inestimable value. Video is used in the training of doctors and nurses and training in any job or profession has been enhanced by the use of videotape to show real situations. Again, this is not new. Film has been used in this way for many years. But what is different about videotape is, firstly its relative cheapness in comparison with film and secondly instant playback. Students can see their own performances recorded on tape straightaway.

The latest developments in the use of videotape in training have been in interactive video, a process which incorporates computer assisted learning and computer assisted training with videos made on tape.

But videotape is not confined to training. Local government record the changing face of architecture and environment on tape; the findings of archaeologists are recorded; conservationists use videotape to provide an archive of specific areas of natural beauty under threat and in furtherance of their cause; and in sales promotion and marketing, videotape has made enormous headway. How often, for example, does one go into a shop to find a group of customers watching a monitor displaying an advertisement? Video has entered virtually every stream of life.

Does the non-broadcast PA exist?

In this burgeoning market covering such a wide field, is an animal such as a PA a necessity to any video production? Does she even exist outside television? Well of course in many areas where video is used, there is no need of a PA. There might be no need for a director either.

'Video has entered virtually every stream of life.'

The simpler the use to which video is put the less need there is for a PA. In some non-broadcast areas the PA exists in the form of a secretary, general dogsbody and 'go-fer'. Sometimes the PA forms part of a company for whom the video unit is only one small section. The PA might exist under other names: production secretary, organizer, secretary and so on. Sometimes the PA is a freelance, employed specifically for a complex production. The needs vary. But in two areas at least there is a kind of hybrid PA and these areas we shall examine next.

Industrial training

Much of industry would go to a production company for their video training needs. They would give the company the brief, work closely on the scripting and provide the locations and facilities necessary for the shooting. The production company would employ a freelance PA as required.

But there are some large companies whose video output is so great they have their own 'in-house' units, making training videos as required for the company. Some of these units are quite large and employ their own full-time PAs; more usually freelance PAs are employed for a specific job.

What sort of work would the PA be expected to do?

The system

Every large company has its own style, its own way of doing things. This is true in television as well as other industries. Therefore the PA working in a video unit within a large industrial company will have to find out the system for getting things done and conform to it. It should not be too difficult as each company generally has written instructions pertaining to its system.

Large companies tend to be self-contained worlds with complex administrative procedures and it is of the first importance that the PA learns what these are. For example, booking overseas accommodation might be done through a network of overseas offices rather than in an ad hoc way.

Corporate image

Another thing the PA must remember is that the company will have its corporate image and that factors such as presentation, how you deal with people, public relations, even the way you and the crew dress will have a certain importance. Although, having said that, you must also remember that industry's perception of film or video units will be somewhat stereotyped and they might expect you to behave or dress in a more unconventional way than you would normally – you are, after all, 'artistic people'!

Different pressures

The time-scale for making industrial videos is different from making programmes for television. You are not working to meet a transmission deadline therefore the feeling is more relaxed, more concerned to get it right. But there are other pressures nonetheless.

For example, if you have arranged an interview with the chairman of the company, being such a highly paid individual, his time is precious and you come very low down on the scale of his priorities. Therefore the pressure will be to cut down on the time you have to interview him.

The priority is not the making of training videos, however worthwhile they are. The priority is the industry itself, whether it is banking, retailing, car manufacture or whatever. So there will always be the frustration of knowing that you are low down on *anyone's* list of priorities.

'You are, after all, "artistic people!"'

Unlimited budgets?

Because we are in general talking about multi-million pound companies, most people labour under the delusion of unlimited multi-million pound budgets and their eyes gleam at the thought of making videos under such conditions.

The truth is far removed. Videos are made to a specific budget in industry as anywhere else and the PA is responsible there as everywhere for the day to day float.

Variety of videos

The videos made can be of any duration. They can be made about all kinds of subjects, the selection following giving some idea of the scope and range of possible training videos:

- [ ] marketing
- [ ] planning
- [ ] training for work in any area of the company
- [ ] public affairs
- [ ] the chairman's report
- [ ] product launches
- [ ] research being undertaken
- [ ] conferences
- [ ] message to staff
- [ ] safety procedures
- [ ] marketing strategies
- [ ] personnel, i.e. job evaluation
- [ ] recruitment.

How videos originate

If a department wants a video made, a series of meetings will be held to get a clear idea of precisely what is needed. A director is brought in at an early stage, usually freelance. Sometimes a PA does not get engaged until quite late in the setting up, so the director will overlap the PA's work.

Words are more important than pictures therefore more time is given to getting the script right and the script approval process takes a long time.

However once the script is finalized and the dates arranged for the shoot, the PA is brought in.

The PA's job

The PA will be responsible for setting up the shoot. She will book the crew (free-lance most probably), arrange travel, book accommodation. She might have to book artists but most likely that would have been done by the director if, indeed, artists are to be involved. The PA will work out the call sheets and the schedule in conjunction with the director and will type and distribute them.

Research

Because there is usually only the director and the PA at work on the setting up, the PA might well find herself involved in research relating to the video content. Some of the research might involve highly confidential matters within the company and therefore discretion is absolutely essential. Sometimes the research might involve simply finding archive film, music and so on.

Overseas locations

If locations are selected overseas, an important aspect of the PA's job will be in the preparation of the 'carnet'. The carnet is a detailed list for customs of all stock and equipment being taken abroad. A number of copies are required and pro forma invoices for consumables, i.e. tapes and batteries, are also necessary.

On location

If the shoot is on location it will undoubtedly be single camera. If there is a studio either single or multi-camera will be used.

On location the PA acts as the 'go-fer'. She will log the shots, perhaps do simple continuity and provide an accurate shot description. Because only small crews tend to be employed, the PA would also do any necessary make-up, get coffee, arrange meals, keep people happy and sort out problems. She will hold the float and pay for accommodation, meals and travel. She will keep a note of the hours worked by the crew and she might well have to acquire props and costume. She will, in fact, do everything and anything necessary at the time.

Studio work

If the company has a television studio the PA will most probably make up the time code log for editing. She might well have to type and operate the teleprompt machine. As with location work, the job will require flexibility and adaptability

'She will hold the float and pay for accommodation, meals and travel.'

and there are not the strict job definitions that mark the mainstream television industry. In that sense a PA can get a lot out of the job and it becomes very much what she chooses to make it.

Post production

The PA would not normally be involved in the editing. After the recording the PA would send out 'thank you' letters, return any captions used, any archive film, props, costumes and so on. She would arrange for any transfers, i.e. of film to videotape. Copyright clearance would form a large part of her work.

Finally, the PA would ensure that the correct number of copies of the finished video were made. The numbers would vary. For a simple recording of a conference perhaps only one copy would be required for the chairman and two for the archives. But for a training or marketing programme the numbers might run into hundreds.

Education
The role of the PA

Despite video being used so extensively in education, it is hard to be specific about the role of the PA. The person doing the job might well have other responsibilities, her main occupation being that of secretary to the producer or head of the video unit.

In a small unit there might only be herself and a producer. She would therefore be at the heart of any production, totally involved in every aspect. Anything that needed doing would therefore be shared between the producer and PA.

Studio work

The PA might be required to do standard gallery work but she might equally well find that during a studio she was required to act as floor manager as well as provide any make-up, costumes or props necessary. She might operate the teleprompt machine, type the camera script, make notes during the studio and provide an assembly for editing. The producer would direct, vision mix and do any necessary cueing and timing.

Location work

When shooting on location the PA would do the more traditional jobs of shot listing and continuity as well as taking responsibility for props, costume and make-up.

Public relations

A vital part of her work would involve dealing with people: with academics, with students, with professional people, with members of the public. Her suitability for the job would tend to be more dependent upon that aspect of her work rather than on the specific skills required in broadcast television.

Types of production

There is no limit to the range of productions that can be made – other than cost and resources – but the types can roughly be divided into two sections: those providing a service for the educational institute and those which could be classed as commercial contracts.

Academic productions

The demand would originate from the tutors and the aim would be to make recordings which are aids to teaching. The academic would ask the unit to make a programme on whatever subject, the script would be the responsibility of the academic and a series of planning meetings with the producer and PA would be held to work out the details.

Many of the productions required would be simply to record lectures for posterity. Many tutorials are now recorded on videotape, using a single camera and with no editing.

Recorded interviews might be asked for. These interviews would be with various 'experts', whose views could materially aid the teaching of whatever subject is involved. The interviews would be recorded in a studio, 'as directed' and with no editing. How the final recording is afterwards used in teaching is up to the tutors: the aim is not to achieve a polished interview within a predetermined duration but to preserve on tape everything that was said by the interviewee.

More ambitious programmes could be and are undertaken. These could range from a full-scale drama production to a publicity film or a set-up 'mock' trial for law students.

The unit might also provide a service that students can use, i.e. viewing facilities, a tape library, the provision of portable equipment, even a studio for use on a self-access basis. Where film and television courses are run by colleges and universities, the facilities would be used to give students varied studio experience and teach them the basics of television and film production.

Commercial contracts

Some colleges undertake commercial contracts that are strictly non-broadcast, providing they do not conflict with the required academic production work. These productions usually have a strong academic content and are often of a training character, i.e. 'How to handle the media' courses for local government personnel, educational programmes of a medical nature, the training of social workers through set up situations and so on.

'These productions usually have a strong academic content.'

Part Five

All you ever wanted to know about videotape but were afraid to ask ...

13

The PA's guide to videotape

A videotape recorder is a machine capable of recording television pictures and sound onto magnetic tape in much the same way as the conventional audio tape recorder. However, videotape recording is very much more complicated than sound recording.

For a start, because the amount of information contained in a colour television picture is infinitely greater than in a piece of recorded sound, if a video recorder had a fixed head as in an audio recorder, it would be necessary for the tape to pass the heads at an impossibly high speed. This problem is overcome by using rotating heads which can scan at high speed across the tape. The tape itself can then move comparatively slowly. The manner in which the heads scan the tape forms the fundamental difference between transverse and helical scan machines.

Various recording systems not only utilize the different scanning arrangements but also use different widths of tape, none of which might be compatible. Narrower tape systems are cheaper to run and provide lightweight, more compact equipment.

There are in existence quite a bewildering array of videotape sizes and formats and the situation is not made any easier by television companies using different names to explain what is essentially the same system.

So it is not just a question of knowing what options are available for recording, the PA must also know what systems are compatible.

In this chapter I have attempted to group the most widely used forms of videotape into simple sections to provide an easy guide for the least technical PA.

Sizes and formats of videotape

2 inch quadruplex (transverse scan)

This has been the standard tape used for broadcasting throughout the world. Its basic problem is that there is no form of still frame or slow replay. In editing therefore one can only see pictures when the tape is running at its correct speed which makes sophisticated editing and fine adjustments very difficult.

The Quad system is being rapidly superseded throughout the industry by:

1 inch videotape (helical scan)

This allows for still frame and slow speed replay and has become the standard tape for broadcast use.

³⁄₄ inch high band videotape

The size of tape is ³⁄₄ inch and is known as 'High Band U-matic'. It is of broadcast quality. It comes in cassette form and the location recorder is easily carried on the shoulder. Its most general application is for ENG (Electronic News Gathering), but ³⁄₄ inch is often used for EFP (Electronic Field Production) and PSC (Portable Single Camera), using high quality cameras. A more recent development is 'SP U-matic' – sometimes known as Super High Band.

³⁄₄ inch low band videotape

The size of tape is ³⁄₄ inch, as in high band, and comes in identical cassettes but the tape is not of broadcast quality. High band and low band systems are not interchangeable although cassettes of either systems can be played back in the machines of the other system for viewing pupposes only. Either way round, the picture is in black and white.

Low band is used:

- [ ] in non-broadcast video
- [ ] in off-line editing (where the master tape, often 1 inch, is transferred to a poorer quality tape for initial editing)
- [ ] for viewing and exhibition purposes, i.e. press shows and sound dubbing, when a higher quality picture than that of a domestic video recorder is required without using expensive broadcast quality equipment.

¹⁄₂ inch broadcast quality videotape

This is used in broadcast quality systems such as Betacam. By using ¹⁄₂ inch tape the recorder can be built into the camera giving a shooting flexibility that is more akin to film.

The advent of higher quality systems such as Sony Betacam SP and Panasonic MII should give the same flexibility allied to performance comparable with 1 inch systems.

¹⁄₂ inch domestic videotape

Other than Betacam, ¹⁄₂ inch tape is most widely found in domestic home video systems which are, however, also used as cheap office viewing and for off-line editing in broadcast companies.

The two main systems in current use are:

- [ ] Video Home System (VHS)
- [ ] Betamax

These systems are not compatible although all use ¹⁄₂ inch tape.

Having said that the domestic systems and low band are of non-broadcast quality, if the shots are of sufficient dramatic interest and unrepeatable in a news sense, then they can be and have been used.

Television systems throughout the world

In addition to the differing tape widths and formats, television systems throughout the world are not standard. There are basically three colour systems in the world. There is the 625 line PAL system, used in the UK and Europe (excepting France), Australia and China; the 525 line NTSC system, used in the USA and Japan; and the 625 line SECAM system, used in France and the USSR.

Material recorded on one television *system* as opposed to *format* is not compatible with another system even if the make and type of machine is the same, unless the material is played through a standards converter.

With cable and satellite and the general opening out of television in the UK has come a world-wide marketing and exchange of programmes. While this would not concern the PA working in any of the large television companies, it is important for PAs in smaller ones and especially those working in satellite and cable to appreciate these differences.

Television systems throughout the world

In addition to the differing tape width and format, television systems throughout the world are not standard. There are basically three colour systems in the world. There is the 625-line PAL system, used in the UK and Europe (excepting France, Australia and China), the 525-line NTSC system, used in the USA and Japan, and the 625-line SECAM system, used in France and the USSR.

Material recorded on one television system as opposed to another is not compatible with another system even if the make and type of machine is the same, unless the material is played through a standards-converter.

With cable and satellite and the general opening out of television in the 1980s, some a world-wide proffering and exchange of programmes. While this would not concern the majority of the larger television companies it is meant to the PAS in smaller uses and especially those working in multi-camera and outside broadcasts where these features

Index

Accommodation, 155
Air timing, 48
Analogue stopwatches, 45
Artists, 106, 147, 155, 160
Artists' chart, 96
Artists' fees, 174
'As directed' sequences, 59, 121, 150
Assistant floor manager, 94
Audience *See* Studio audience

Back timing, 30
Band calls, 149
Bar counting, 148
Billings, 176
Blocking, 109
Buffer items, 26, 30

Cable television, 184
Camera, 132
   cards, 126, 129
   mountings, 132
   movements, 124
   numbers, 118
   operators, 63, 137
   positions, 109, 118
   rehearsal, 133
   script, 36, 109, 111, 128, 149
   terms, 123
Capgens, 14, 24, 37, 54, 57
Captions, 14, 129
Carnet, 197
Cassette numbers, 163
Cast lists, 107, 113
Casting director, 95
Catering, 156
Check lists, 90
Children, 107, 174
Clearing up, 173
Clerks, 17
Co-productions, 176
Colour coding, 98
Command words. 56
Commentary, 172
Commentators, 66

Commercial breaks, 30, 57
Commercials, 187, 189
Communications, 65
Computers, 14, 16, 19, 125
Conferences, 19
Continuity, 157
Copyright, 104, 174
Costume
   notes, 160
   supervisors, 95, 103
Countdowns, 37, 48, 58
Counting in/out, 37, 44, 52, 53, 58
Coverage script, 145, 164
Creative sequences, 14
Crossing the line, 160
Cue dots, 56
Cueing, 35, 44, 54, 56
Cut line, 118

Day by day chart, 96
Designer, 93
Director, 17, 59, 63, 93, 154, 162
Discussion, studio-based, 58
Distribution lists, 91, 98
Dub, 168
Dub editing, 166
Durations, 21, 26, 147

Editing, 60, 164
   facilities, booking, 170
   off/on-line, 168, 169
Education: videotape, 199
End credits, 14, 50
Ending programmes, 49
Equipment in a live studio, 41
Extras (walk-ons), 106, 155

Facility houses, 183
Film
   conforming, 169
   editing, 166
   inserts, 13, 104, 121, 174
   leaders, 52, 54

Finance, 105, 174, 189, 196
Fixed duration items, 26
Floater, 29
Floor assistant, 94
Floor manager, 93
Floor plans, 24, 109
Forms, 102, 105, 173
Forward timing, 30
Framing, 158, 162
Freelance, 181

Gallery *See* Studio gallery
Graphic designer, 95, 104
Graphics, 13, 24, 125, 129

Hazards *See* Job hazards

Ident, 52, 54
Industrial training: videotape, 195
Injects *See* Live injects
Inserts, 12, 23, 53, 54, 56, 121, 174
Interviews, studio-based, 58, 164

Job hazards, 77
Job responsibilities, 10, 42, 102
Journalists, 17, 23

Layout of camera scripts, 34
Lettering, 14
Liaison, 24, 65
Light entertainment, 145
Lighting, 131
Live injects, 13
Live programme, 10
   problems, 79
   studio, 40
Location
   details, 163
   manager, 91, 155
   work, 154, 197, 198, 199

Make-up supervisors, 95, 103
Meetings, 19, 103, 155
Minute warnings, 42
Monitors, 53, 138, 152, 153
Multi-camera shooting, 86
Music, 104, 129, 145, 148, 171, 174
   pre-fading, 50

News script, 32
Newsreader, 12

Newsroom
   daily schedule, 19
   organization, 16
Note taking, 134

Observation, 158
One minute clock, 50
Opting, 30
Organizers, 17
Outside broadcasts, 61
   schedules, 100

Page numbering of news script, 34
Paperwork, 87
Personnel in live studio, 41
Personnel lists, 90, 129
Petty cash, 156
Photocalls, 107, 113
Planning meetings, 103
Pop promotions, 187, 188
Post production, 176, 188, 199
Presenter, 12, 56, 57
Previewing, 44, 52, 138
Producer, 16, 48, 92
Producer's run, 110
Production
   associate, 92
   buyer, 95
   companies, 183
   list, 96
   manager, 93
   numbers, 90
   secretary, 95
   team, 92
Promotions *See* Pop promotions
Properties, 103, 160
   buyer, 95
Public relations, 189, 199
Publicity, 176

Queries, 134

Read-through, 108, 140
Real time, 46, 153
Record of shooting, 164
Recorded music, 129
Recording breaks, 119
Recording log, 144
Recording order, 102, 113, 128
Reel numbers, 163, 168
Rehearsal, 42, 58, 108, 133, 155
   schedules, 100
   scripts, 97, 128
Reporters, 17
Roll cues, 35
Rolling, 44, 54

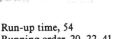

Run-up time, 54
Running order, 20, 22, 41

Satellite broadcasting, 185
Scenes, 95, 117, 121
Schedules, 19, 100, 113, 156
Screen direction, 158
Scripts, 95, 147
  breakdown, 98
  changes, 134
  check, 42
  editors, 92
  marking, 34
  See also Camera scripts
Sequences, 20
Sets, 131
Shots, 158
  calling, 137
  descriptions, 118, 123, 163
  identification, 163
  lists, 163
  numbers, 118
Single camera shooting, 86, 152, 163
Sketches, 162
Sound, 123, 124, 129, 133, 170
Source of news items, 21
Source sheets, 37, 41
Sports events, 65
Stage manager, 94
Stagger through, 133
Standbys, 23, 37, 44, 54
Stopwatches, 41, 45, 129
Story editor, 92
Studio
  audience, 104, 113, 147
  call sheets, 107, 128
  day facilities, 104
  floor, 24, 109, 130

Studio (*cont.*)
  gallery, 40, 68, 133, 152
  schedules, 113
  work: non-broadcast, 198, 199
Stuntmen, 106

Takes, 164
Talkback system, 41
Technical run, 110
Telecine bookings, 104
Teleprompt operator, 17, 24
Televison systems, world, 207
Time charts, 27, 41, 49, 129
Time code, 142, 166
  tape running time, 142
  logging, 141, 153
  time of day, 143
Time sheets, 107
Timing, 26, 43, 48, 65, 108, 140, 147, 164
Training of PAs, 181
Transmission Controllers, 186
Transmission form, 176
Transparencies, 129
Typists, 19

Unscripted programmes, 163

Video conforming, 169
Videotape
  editing, 164, 167, 170
  inserts, 13, 121, 174
  non-broadcast use, 193
  recording bookings, 104
  research, 197
  size and format, 205
Vision mixing, 63, 125